To my parents

Who inspire me by their faith in God
Who refresh me by their confidence in my abilities
Who model faithfulness by their enduring love

1 Searching for Faith

I remember distinctly when I began my search for faith. I was 14 years old and I knew I had some faith because I was a Christian, and the Bible teaches that the only way a person can become a Christian is by faith. But then something happened in my life that convinced me I didn't have as much faith as I wanted.

Like many adolescents, I was insecure and inhibited. I didn't talk much and I smiled less than I talked. After my mother made many attempts to find out why I was so shy and gloomy, I finally broke down and explained it to her. The main problem was my teeth. They were crooked and crowded, and I was embarrassed for people to see them. Since talking and smiling meant exposing my teeth, I simply avoided both.

After my painful revelation a family conference was held and the decision made for me to get braces. I was glad that finally something was going to be done about my teeth, but less than thrilled with the thought of wearing braces just as I was going into high school. From years of Sunday School lessons and memorizing Bible verses, I remembered some of the promises Jesus made about prayer. To refresh my memory and to make sure that I hadn't misunderstood, I took out my Bible and looked up these verses:

• "Until now you have asked for nothing in My name; ask, and you will receive, that your joy may be made full" (John 16:24).

• "Truly, truly, I say to you, he who believes in Me, the works that I do shall he do also; and greater works than these shall he do; because I go to the Father. And whatever you ask in My name, that will I do, that the Father may be glorified in the Son. If you ask Me anything in My name, I will do it" (John 14:12-14).

• "Truly I say to you, whoever says to this mountain, 'Be taken up and cast into the sea,' and does not doubt in his heart, but believes that what he says is going to happen, it shall be granted him. Therefore I say to you, all things for which you pray and ask, believe that you have received them, and they shall be granted you" (Mark 11:23-24).

It seemed pretty clear to me. If I asked in faith that God would straighten my teeth, He would do it. I could see no value in going through the bother of braces. They would mean financial hardship to our family and would cause me a great deal of discomfort. And if I was too shy to smile with crooked teeth, I was quite sure I wouldn't smile with "tinsel teeth."

Just to make sure that it was OK to ask God to do such a thing for me, I asked my brother what he thought. Dave knew the Bible better than I did, and since he was older, I trusted his word completely. When I explained what I planned to ask God to do, and showed him the verse on which I based my plan, Dave hesitated for a moment and then agreed it would be a valid request to make. That was all I needed to hear!

That night, less than 24 hours before I was to go in to be measured for braces, I prayed as I had never prayed before. Never before had I felt so confident that God would answer my prayers. Jesus had said that if I just had faith, He would grant the request I made of Him. My faith was unshakable. I was totally convinced that when I woke up in the morning my teeth would be as straight and even as the keyboard of a piano. If God could move mountains, then straightening a few teeth shouldn't be any problem at all!

The next morning, I jumped out of bed, hurried to the bathroom, and confidently grinned at the scrawny, sleepy figure in the mirror. To my amazement, nothing had changed. Every tooth was just where it had been the night before. But why? I knew other people who had prayed for miracles that seemed much more difficult than what I had asked and had received amazing answers to their prayers. In my mind there seemed to be only one explanation—I simply didn't have enough faith.

Have you ever known a person who seemed to be able to get from God just what he asked for? For much of my life, being a person of faith meant praying for something and getting that very thing. My belief in that definition of faith was reinforced by people I read about or heard speak, and by people I knew personally who seemed to have just the kind of faith I wanted. I read about missionaries who prayed in faith for protection, wisdom, opportunities, healing, and finances, and who seemingly got everything they prayed for. I heard pastors and seminar speakers relate amazing stories of how God answered their prayers because of their faith. One speaker explained how early in his ministry he needed $96 to continue with his seminars. He prayed in faith and, sure enough, the $96 came in the mail from two anonymous donors on the exact day he needed it. Three years later he needed $200,000 to purchase some property that would greatly benefit his ministry. He prayed in faith and, sure enough, on the exact day he needed the money, checks totaling $200,000 arrived in the mail.

The heroes of faith I most admired, though, were my own grandparents. For years they had been traveling evangelists and church planters, and they had story after story of God's faithful answers to their prayers to share with their wide-eyed grandchildren. One summer, they were traveling across some high elevations in their old Buick. The car was overdue for retirement, but somehow Grandpa kept it going because they needed it for their ministry and couldn't afford to buy another one. On this trip the car was overheating. Every few miles they had to pour some water into the radiator to keep the engine functioning.

Grandpa had promised the people in the next town that he would be there that day to begin his evangelistic meetings, and as a stubborn Norwegian he took that promise very seriously. As the day wore on and their bottled water ran out, it seemed inevitable that the car was going to overheat and break down, stranding my grandparents, my mother, and my mother's sister in the middle of nowhere.

So Grandpa did what he always did in those situations. He got out of the car and prayed that God would provide them with more water so that they could keep the car running and reach their destination. He got back in the car and began coasting it down a hill. Out of the corner of her eye my grandmother spotted something shiny off to the side of the road. Grandpa stopped the car again and ran over to get a closer look. As he approached, he saw it was a large container, filled to the brim with water! After stopping to thank God for hearing his prayer, Grandpa poured some of the water into the radiator and refilled the empty jars he had in the trunk. Grandpa and his family arrived for their next tent meeting right on schedule.

I couldn't even get God to straighten out my teeth! If only I had more faith!

What Is Faith?

Since that episode about my teeth, I have had many more experiences of much greater consequence in which my prayers of faith have seemed inadequate. When one of my childhood friends was diagnosed with cancer, I prayed with faith for his healing. He died in less than a year. When my father had a heart attack, my mother and I prayed with faith for his total recovery. When he came home after three weeks in the hospital we thanked God for answering our prayers. We never doubted that within a short time our lives would be back to normal. Three days after he returned home, my father died.

Now as a pastor I am brought face to face with circumstances of major importance in the lives of church members. They come to me in the hope that my prayers of faith will make a difference. They look to me to give them encouragement and assurance that all will be well again. In faith I pray for a new job for a father who has been laid off after 23 years on the job. In faith I pray with a high schooler whose parents bicker constantly and frequently threaten to throw her out of the house. In faith I pray with a woman dying from cancer and with her frightened husband. In faith I pray with the leaders of our church for the church to grow and for our financial needs to be met.

Often those prayers are answered. Often they are not. And when the prayers aren't answered, not only do I grope for the reasons to satisfy myself, but now the people with whom I've prayed come to me for answers. They want to know why a husband died or why parents broke up after they prayed with such complete faith in God.

In order to better answer those questions, I set out to do

a thorough study of faith. I began by reexamining key biblical passages that teach us about faith.

I also thought it would be wise to find out from other people what they have learned about faith. So I devised a questionnaire, gave it to people from various churches representing different aspects of the theological and vocational spectrum, and then spent an hour with each person, listening to what he had learned about faith. The eight questions I asked were:

• What is your personal definition of faith? How might you describe, explain, or illustrate faith?

• How has faith affected the way you live?

• Has there ever been a particular time in your life when you sensed that your faith was especially strong and alive? What was that like? How did you judge the strength and vitality of your faith? Why do you think your faith was stronger during that particular time?

• Do you think it is possible for a person to actively strengthen, increase, or develop his faith? If so, what action steps might he employ?

• Jesus told His disciples, "And whatever you ask in prayer, you will receive, if you have faith" (Matt. 21:22, RSV). What does that verse mean to you? What do you think Jesus was trying to teach His disciples?

• Imagine that you are introduced to someone who is known to be a person of faith. In terms of the way you understand faith, what would that person be like?

• Suppose that you are praying for God to perform a miracle, one that you believe would be glorifying to Him. The Bible teaches that one requirement for prayer to be answered is that you have faith. Do you think this means you are required to have faith that God *can* do the miracle for which you are praying? Or to have faith that God *will* perform the miracle? Or does the Bible mean something else?

• Have you or has anyone you know personally ever had an answer to prayer that seemed especially meaningful or unusual? Could you describe it briefly?

After conducting only a few interviews, I was startled to discover how limited a concept of faith I had. I had viewed faith as having two main functions—through faith I could experience salvation and through faith I could receive answers to my prayers. But I learned that faith offers us much more! Certainly there is no more important value of faith than to experience a personal relationship with God through Jesus Christ. Yet once that relationship has begun, faith offers us much more than clout with God so that we can get from Him what we want.

A Person of Faith

When I was 14 I wanted to grow my faith in order to get my teeth straightened. Today I still want a mature faith, but my reasons are much different. I want to enjoy a deeper intimacy with God. I want to become a person who refreshes and inspires the people around me. I want to become a person of faith so that I will be able to endure hardship and find meaning and comfort in pain. I want faith so that when God calls me to take a risk, in order to accomplish something significant in our world, I'll be ready to jump.

I want to become a person of faith because I want to be like Jesus Christ. That is also why *God* wants me to become a person of faith. That is also why God wants *you* to become a person of faith. Let the search begin! Let's grow our faith!

In the following chapters, we will be looking at four areas related to faith.

The first is a definition of faith. Definitions that seem cold and dormant can come to life when we take time to understand what they mean. Then we will look at ways in which faith is valuable for our everyday lives. A person of faith is a person with an effective prayer life, but he is also much more. A person of faith is free from worry, anxiety, and insecurity. A person of faith has strength to endure and to persist through any adversity. A person of faith is adventuresome and daring. His vision makes him a vital force in changing the shape of his world. A person of faith refreshes and invigorates the people around him with his energy and optimism.

We want to examine why faith does not always move the mountain, and to suggest factors that limit faith's power. In connection with this we will consider the subject of doubt.

Then we will illustrate how we can grow our faith. Just as with our muscles and our abilities, we must develop our faith or it will atrophy. Our bodies grow and our muscles develop as we provide them with the proper nutrients and exercise. If we give our faith the right ingredients and exercise it regularly, it too can grow.

2 | What Is Faith?

Many of the theological words most important to Christians often strike us as cold, ethereal concepts. Words such as predestination, sovereignty, sanctification, immanence, and propitiation may wash over us like a spray of icy ocean water, leaving us numb.

But *faith* is not one of those words. Faith does not float haphazardly in space waiting to be bottled and analyzed. Faith has substance. It bleeds when we cut it. For faith is able to exist only in the shape of a human being. It is a word with a face.

Even more, faith is a power with ability to transform human faces. Faith transforms the face of despair into hope, the face of fear into courage, and the face of timidity into boldness. Faith erases the lines of worry and anxiety that wrinkle our lives, and leaves us confident and serene.

It is by faith that our sins are forgiven and we are restored to a right relationship with God. It is by faith that we are delivered from the penalty and power of sin. It is by faith that people whose lives have been shattered by despair, anxiety, and loneliness are reclaimed, repaired, and resurrected through the power of God.

Since Martin Luther's *Ninety-Five Theses* in 1517, there has been little argument with the statement that a person is saved by faith. The New Testament letters of Paul resonate with this truth.

• "For by grace you have been saved through faith; and that not of yourselves, it is the gift of God; not as a result of works, that no one should boast" (Eph. 2:8-9).

• "For we maintain that a man is justified by faith apart from works of the Law" (Rom. 3:28).

• "Therefore the Law has become our tutor to lead us to Christ, that we may be justified by faith. But now that faith has come, we are no longer under a tutor. For you are all sons of God through faith in Christ Jesus" (Gal. 3:24-26).

Because it is by faith alone that a person is saved, faith is one of the most important words in the vocabulary of the Christian. Yet while we live by faith and know God through faith, defining it is about as easy as drinking ice. Yet it is only as we define faith that it can begin to live and breathe through our experience.

As I interviewed people and pulled together some of the biblical passages that illustrate faith, I saw three components that relate to three aspects of our humanness—intellect, emotion, and will. Faith speaks to what we believe, how we feel, and what we do.

Some individuals I interviewed described their faith primarily in terms of what they believed, others of how they felt, and still others of what they did. The Bible affirms that all three components—how we believe, feel, and act—are vital to a complete understanding of faith.

Faith as Belief

The first aspect of faith taught in the Bible usually goes by
the name *belief*. The dictionary defines *belief* as being "convinced by argument or evidence that certain things are true."
For the Christian, faith as belief means to be convinced
intellectually that those historical events and spiritual concepts declared in the Bible are true.

Some of us have been told by well-meaning people that
the intellect really isn't important when it comes to faith.
When I was in college and wrestling with intellectual questions concerning my faith, there were Christians who responded to my questions by saying, "You know, the important
thing isn't that you have the answers to all your questions.
The important thing is that you believe. If you will just have
faith, your life will be changed." Then they would share
with me their personal experience with Jesus Christ and
how He had changed their lives.

While I appreciated what they had to say, I always left
those conversations feeling that I had been talking to people
who didn't want to address my questions. I was very un-
satisfied, and began to wonder if perhaps there weren't any
answers.

It was then that I had the opportunity of spending a
weekend at a retreat with the late Paul Little. The first message he gave was just what I needed to assuage my rising
doubts. One illustration in particular assured me that it wasn't
unreasonable for me to ask intellectual questions.

Paul Little asked us to imagine a worship service during
which a man walked to the front of the sanctuary and began
to address the congregation. On top of this man's head was
a fried egg. He told us that ever since he had put that fried
egg on top of his head, his life had been radically changed.
Now he was pleading with us to wear fried eggs on our
heads and to give up our belief in Jesus Christ. When we

asked him what reasons he had for believing that the fried egg had some power to change his life, he would only reply that it wasn't necessary to understand how the fried egg worked, as long as you believed in it.

"Don't we as Christians do the same thing," asked Paul Little, "when we tell the non-Christian that it isn't as important to answer his questions as to sincerely believe? Aren't we giving people the impression that faith is irrational? That experience matters more than rational belief?"

As Paul Little explained that day, faith does involve the intellect. Because believing something does not make it true, *what* we believe and *why* we believe what we do are of the utmost importance. Believing that a fried egg can give us supernatural power does not make it true. But neither does simply believing in the resurrection of Christ make that true. And if Christ did not rise from the dead, then our believing that He did won't do us any good at all. As Paul said, "And if Christ has not been raised, then our preaching is vain, your faith also is vain" (1 Cor. 15:14).

As Christians we are not asked to just believe, as if believing something without knowing much about it is more spiritual than believing something after having asked 50 questions. Rather, we are asked to decide on the basis of evidence whether or not we will believe, for example, that Jesus Christ did rise from the dead.

Faith is not a blind leap in the dark but is based on solid evidence. Christian faith is not without reason. There are many good reasons to believe what the Bible teaches. Neither does Christian faith go against reason. Faith is not, as has been facetiously suggested, believing something we know isn't true. Christian faith is reasonable. And while the evidence for our faith is not exhaustive, it is sufficient.

Yet Christian faith also goes beyond reason. Much of what we believe as Christians cannot be seen or measured.

We are asked by the Bible to believe things for which there can never be incontrovertible and scientifically validated proof. The existence of God, life after death, the power of the blood of Jesus Christ to cleanse a person from the guilt of sin, and the indwelling of the Holy Spirit are realities insisted on by Scripture, and for which there can never be full proof. The fact that God's existence cannot be verified by observable data is not in itself an insoluble problem, since there are many realities, such as pain, that we accept without observable proof. But the Christian must go beyond his reason, not against it, in choosing to believe and accept what the Bible teaches to be true.

In order to be saved, to be forgiven of our sin and to enter into a right relationship with God, we must first of all believe in certain truths. Hebrews 11:6 tells us, "And without faith it is impossible to please Him, for he who comes to God must believe that He is, and that He is a rewarder of those who seek Him."

In the first chapter of his Gospel, the Apostle John specified what we must believe in order to be saved: "But as many as received Him [Jesus Christ], to them He gave the right to become children of God, even to those who believe in His name" (John 1:12). Believing in the name of Jesus means believing what Jesus claimed about Himself.

In his first letter, John made sure his readers would understand that the message he preached was not something he made up:

> We write to you about the Word of life, which has existed from the very beginning. We have heard it, and we have seen it with our eyes; yes, we have seen it, and our hands have touched it. When this life became visible, we saw it; so we speak of it and tell you about the eternal life which was with the Father and was made known to us (1 John 1:1-2, GNB).

John made it clear that he had solid, tangible evidence for believing that Jesus Christ lived and died as a real human being. As Paul pointed out, in 1 Corinthians 15:1-4, the essentials that we must accept as true are: that Jesus Christ lived, that He died for our sins, that He was buried, and that He physically rose from the dead on the third day.

Faith that saves is faith that believes. It is a faith that is convinced intellectually by the available evidence that what the Bible teaches about God, about sin, and about Jesus Christ is true. Faith involves our minds.

Faith as Feeling

Faith also involves our emotions. Many of the people I interviewed described faith as a confidence, an assurance, a feeling that God is there and is good. Some reported this feeling as a sensation that God was so near to them they could almost reach out and take His hand.

In order to be saved, a person does not have to be overpowered by the feeling of faith. The Bible never commands us to "feel" trusting or to "sense" God's presence. Yet God has created us as emotional beings, and it is right for our feelings to be responsive to Him.

Hebrews 11:1 acknowledges the feeling component of faith: "Now faith is the assurance of things hoped for, the conviction of things not seen." The Greek word for assurance is *hupostasis*, meaning "a firm confidence." In this respect faith is fairly subjective. It is something we feel, much as we feel joy or sorrow. As such, faith serves as an antidote to worry, anxiety, and doubt.

Others I interviewed described faith as an optimism they feel about the future, or as a cheerfulness and a calm about the present. Some described faith as a feeling of hopefulness, as a confident expectation that everything will turn out for the best.

Almost everyone I asked about faith used the word *trust* in their description. Most of them defined trust as a confidence that God will do what He has promised to do. And they emphasized that the object of their trust was not a set of beliefs, an institution, or a code of ethics, but a Person— God.

While *faith* and *trust* are to some extent synonymous, for most of us *trust* has come to represent that intangible bond of loyalty, that sense of oneness between two people. When I say that I trust my wife, I am referring to the strength of our relationship. I depend on her to be available when I need her. Even though I don't know what she is doing every minute of the day, I am confident she will act responsibly and for our best. Because I trust her, I am not suspicious of her, nor do I doubt her word or her motives. I believe *in* my wife.

Dr. Norman Geisler has explained that there is a difference between *belief that* and *belief in*. *Belief that* refers to the intellectual component of faith. *Belief that* demands evidence. In order for me to believe that Jesus Christ rose from the dead, my mind requires that I supply it with reasonable evidence.

Belief in is trust in a person. It does not demand evidence. *Belief in* is to be confident that the other person will act out of pure motives. If I trust someone I will lend him my car without collateral. Because I believe in him, I am confident that I can depend on him to return my car.

In fact, to trust someone means that I will sometimes believe in him *despite* the evidence. There have been occasions when the evidence has seemed to suggest that a friend of mine has not been telling me the truth. Yet if I believe in him I will continue to trust him anyway and to expect that there will be a reasonable explanation which will justify my confidence. And if I trust someone, I will believe in him even if I don't understand the whys behind his actions.

To believe in Jesus Christ is to depend on Him to do what He has said He will do. To be saved by faith is to trust Jesus Christ to forgive my sins and to deliver me from sin's penalty and power. To "walk by faith and not by sight," as Paul puts it, is to trust God to provide for my needs and to work everything—including the bad things—together for good. And because I believe in God, I will continue to trust Him even if I don't understand why He chooses to do what He does.

Because we have been created as feeling beings, faith cannot help but involve our feelings and emotions. While we don't have to feel optimistic, confident, or cheerful in order to be saved, faith often is experienced in those ways.

Faith that saves is faith that trusts. Faith is both a belief *that* Jesus Christ died on the cross for the sins of humanity, and a belief *in* Jesus Christ to forgive my sins. Faith objectively accepts as true what the Bible teaches, and subjectively trusts God to do for me what He has promised in the Bible.

Faith as Action

The third thing that distinguishes saving faith from "useless" faith (James 2:20) is the *action* of faith. While an intellectual belief in God's existence and Christ's resurrection is *necessary*, to have a right relationship with God, it is not *sufficient*. James 2:19 tells us, "You believe that God is one. You do well; the demons also believe, and shudder." Though Satan and the demons believe many of the same things the Christian does about Jesus Christ, their belief does not save them.

Saving faith involves our will as well as our intellect and emotions. Faith that saves is faith that acts, faith that makes an active commitment of one's will to God.

Hebrews 11 illustrates what it means to have faith, in

example after example of people who acted on what they believed and then obeyed the God they trusted.

• "By faith Abel *offered* to God a better sacrifice than Cain, through which he obtained the testimony that he was righteous" (v. 4).

• "By faith Noah, being warned by God about things not yet seen, in reverence *prepared* an ark for the salvation of his household, by which he condemned the world, and became an heir of the righteousness which is according to faith" (v. 7).

• "By faith Abraham, when he was called, *obeyed* by going out to a place which he was to receive for an inheritance; and he went out, not knowing where he was going" (v. 8).

• "By faith Abraham, when he was tested, *offered* up Isaac" (v. 17).

• "It was faith that made Moses, when he had grown up, *refuse* to be called the son of the king's daughter. He preferred to *suffer* with God's people rather than to enjoy sin for a little while. . . . It was faith that made Moses *leave* Egypt without being afraid of the king's anger. As though he saw the invisible God, he refused to turn back" (vv. 24-25, 27, GNB).

We see real faith in action. Abel's faith led him to make an offering. Noah's faith motivated him to spend 120 years building an enormous boat in the middle of a desert. Abraham's faith caused him to pack up all of his belongings, leave the town where he grew up, and head for a place he knew nothing about. By faith Moses turned his back on the good life in the palaces of Egypt and chose instead to identify in suffering with the oppressed people of Israel. Faith that saves is faith that acts.

I believe the greatest single act of faith in the Bible, outside of the life of Jesus Christ, is Abraham's willingness to offer Isaac as a sacrifice. God had promised Abraham that through his son he would become the father of many nations. Isaac was the child of promise, the son for whom Abraham had waited for years. It stretches our faith to think of his being asked to take a knife and plunge it into his son's body to offer him as a sacrifice to God. It goes beyond our comprehension to think of being asked to put to death the very person who had been miraculously born for the purpose of perpetuating our family line.

To bring the story more into our own experience, imagine that my wife is dying from cancer. One day while I am praying fervently to God for her healing, God gives me a promise: "Don't be afraid. I will give you a cure for cancer."

How wonderful! God has promised to give me a cure for a disease that has taken thousands of lives, has baffled doctors, and is threatening Brenda's life. I wait and wait as Brenda struggles against the disease, and then God gives me a serum that will cure Brenda and everyone else with cancer.

Hardly able to control my ecstasy, I run through the halls of the hospital like a greyhound on a racetrack. As I turn the corner to go into Brenda's room, I hear a voice:

"Craig, I want you to destroy the serum."

"What's that, Lord?"

"I said I want you to destroy the serum."

"But, Lord, You promised me this serum to save Brenda and all these other sick people. You aren't going back on Your promise, are You?"

"No, Craig, I'm not going back on My word. I never do that. I can't go back on My word because of My holiness."

"So then You're kidding about destroying the serum?"

"No, I'm not. Destroy the serum."

"Then after I destroy the serum, You'll give me another?"

"No. There will be no other serum. This is it."

"But Lord, I don't understand. If I destroy the serum my wife will die, and so will all these other people."

"Craig, destroy the serum."

"But Lord, it doesn't make sense!"

Just as it wouldn't make sense for me to destroy a serum that could save my wife, I doubt it made sense to Abraham to put Isaac to death. Yet even though he didn't understand, by faith Abraham obeyed God and lowered the knife toward Isaac's body. Hebrews 11:17-19 gives this account of that event:

> It was faith that made Abraham offer his son Isaac as a sacrifice when God put Abraham to the test. Abraham was the one to whom God had made the promise, yet he was ready to offer his only son as a sacrifice. God had said to him, "It is through Isaac that you will have the descendants I promised." Abraham reckoned that God was able to raise Isaac from death—and, so to speak, Abraham did receive Isaac back from death (GNB).

Faith obeys even when it doesn't understand. God rewarded Abraham's faith by sending an angel to stop the knife from puncturing Isaac's heart. As far as Abraham was concerned, he had already killed Isaac in his mind. And his faith in God was so total that, even though he didn't understand why God would command him to do such a thing, he trusted Him to live up to His promise, even if it required raising Isaac from the dead. By faith Abraham obeyed.

What is faith? Faith is acting on unseen truth. Yes, faith accepts intellectually the truth that the God who cannot be seen exists. Faith trusts in God to do what He has promised to do. Then real faith acts on the truth that God exists. If I have this kind of faith, I will live much differently than if I do not. Faith that does not affect what I do is not faith at all. It may be a belief or a strong feeling; but unless it touches my actions and speech, it is not faith.

Bob Thorp believes what the Bible says about the poor, the homeless, and the hungry, and what Jesus taught in Matthew 25—that to feed and clothe the poor is to feed and clothe Jesus Himself. By faith Bob Thorp left the abundance of the United States to live in Somalia where he fed starving children and helped build more efficient stoves for the Somali women to use in cooking. When he left for California, after spending a year coordinating Food for the Hungry's feeding program with the refugees in Somalia, children there were no longer dying from hunger.

Will Bob stay in California now to get a good-paying job and eat steaks and hamburgers? Not a chance. His faith won't let him stay. He'll be gone again in a few weeks to another part of the world to feed the hungry, build shelters for the homeless, and to tell the Gospel to people as hungry for truth and love as they are for food.

> What use is it, my brethren, if a man says he has faith, but he has no works? Can that faith save him? If a brother or sister is without clothing and in need of daily food, and one of you says to them, "Go in peace, be warmed and be filled," and yet you do not give them what is necessary for their body, what use is that? Even so faith, if it has no works, is dead, being by itself (James 2:14-17).

Faith involves the whole person—intellect, emotions, and will. Faith believes intellectually that those historical events and spiritual concepts insisted on by the Bible are true. Faith is a confidence and a trust that God will do what He's promised to do. And faith is acting on unseen truth. Faith obeys, faith serves, faith sacrifices, faith goes.

It is this active faith that is saving faith.

3 Faith and Your Feelings

Though it is certainly true that our feelings are not always dependable, it is also true that life without emotions would be like a world without color. While I am grateful that the status of my marriage and the standing of my salvation do not depend on my vacillating emotions, I am also glad that God has provided a whole spectrum of emotions for me to enjoy within these areas of life.

Try to think of what you would be like without emotions. You wouldn't feel hurt by criticism. You wouldn't be upset when your favorite team lost the championship game. You wouldn't be irritated when another driver cut your car off in traffic. You wouldn't grieve when a close friend died.

Yet, in a world without emotions, you would never feel the satisfaction of accomplishment. You wouldn't laugh at the chimpanzees playing in the zoo. You wouldn't feel the ecstasy of seeing your spouse after one of you had been on a short trip, nor the exhilaration of introducing a friend to Jesus Christ.

Life without emotions would be like a world without

color, like a restaurant with only one item on the menu, like a bakery without aroma, a candy store without chocolate.

It is important to remember that our emotions—all of them—are gifts of God. He has given them to us so that we might enjoy knowing Him, savor our relationships with each other, and take delight in the grandeur and variety of God's creation. It is right for us to value our emotions and to appreciate the flavor and color that they add to our lives.

But emotions, like any good thing, can be given too much rein. If we allow them to, they can dominate us and even terrorize us. They can deceive and mislead us in our decision-making, confuse our motivations, consume our energy, and disrupt the harmony of our relationships.

Good things taken to an extreme are usually destructive. Sleep is a good thing, something we can't live without. But when a person uses sleep as an escape, as a means of avoiding responsibility, sleep becomes unhealthy.

Emotions are good gifts of God. It is healthy to feel grief when a loved one dies. But when a person continues in deep depression 10 years after a spouse has died, grief is destructive.

We need something to moderate our emotions, to temper their intensity, to govern their influence. We need something that will provide stability for our fluctuating feelings. That something is faith.

The Bible teaches that faith has a very important role to play in the regulation of our feelings. Faith is both the *antidote* to our negative emotions and the *activator* of our positive emotions. Let's take a closer look at these two functions of faith.

Antidote to Negative Emotions

What images or words come to your mind when you hear the phrase *negative emotions*? One word leaps immediately to my mind—*pain*. For me, a negative emotion is one which in some way causes pain. Feeling lonely is painful. Feeling disappointed at age 10 because I didn't get the surprise birthday party I was expecting was painful. Feeling anxious about the speech I have to give tomorrow is painful. Feeling hurt by unkind remarks I overheard about myself is painful.

Two of the most common and painful negative emotions are depression and anxiety. We live in what many historians have labeled "the age of anxiety." Psychologist Rollo May suggests that anxiety is one of the most urgent problems of our day. Statistics reveal that 2 million U.S. residents suffer from profound depression and 53 million more suffer from mild to moderate depression. One medical journal proposed that more human suffering has resulted from depression than from any other single source.

What does the Bible have to say about how we handle negative emotions? How does faith function as an antidote to the pain caused by our sensitive feelings?

Jesus told His disciples that the truth would set them free (John 8:32). Just as the truth of the Gospel sets the repentant sinner free from the penalty of sin, so the truth of the Gospel sets the afflicted individual free from the debilitating pain of negative emotions.

The role that faith plays in this process is to enable us to respond appropriately and actively to the truth. Faith acts on unseen truth. Faith gives hands and feet to the truth which liberates us from our pain.

There are certain essential truths taught in the Bible that are able to free us from the blight of our negative emotions. One of these is the truth that pain can be profitable, that God can use our bruises for good.

While we might often wish we lived in a world free from pain, we would actually be much worse off than we are now. A short time ago I spent more time lounging in the sun that I should have. For days afterward, I felt like my skin was tearing away from my bones. Putting on my clothes in the morning became a major ordeal.

Yet if it weren't for that pain, I would have continued to expose myself to the rays of the sun, and my skin could have been permanently damaged. The physical pain I experienced warned me of an even worse danger.

Emotional pain can also be for our ultimate benefit. It can alert us to an inner sickness that needs our attention. Just as the pain of a toothache sends us to a dentist, so emotional pain can impel us to seek out someone to heal our inner infirmity.

It was the pain of intense guilt that drove Augustine to seek the forgiveness of God. Had he not felt that internal anguish, he never would have turned to God. How grateful Augustine must have been that he could feel guilty!

The Bible reminds us that God's highest ambition for us is that we become people of purity and holiness. Over and over again the Bible instructs us that God often uses our pain and anguish to fashion us into the kind of people He wants us to be.

> Before I was afflicted I went astray,
> But now I keep Thy word. . . .
> It is good for me that I was afflicted,
> That I may learn Thy statutes (Ps. 119:67, 71).

> Consider it all joy, my brethren, when you encounter various trials, knowing that the testing of your faith produces endurance. And let endurance have its perfect result, that you may be perfect and complete, lacking in nothing (James 1:2-4).

Yet this truth will be of no benefit to us as long as it remains isolated in the pages of our Bibles. It is only when we respond to that truth by faith that the despair is removed from our pain and we begin to grow. We must believe that God can use our bruises to make us pure.

Anxiety

Faith as an antidote to anxiety is formed in the three-pronged truth that God is sovereign, good, and active. Jesus taught His disciples this truth in the Sermon on the Mount:

> Therefore I tell you, do not be anxious about your life, what you shall eat or what you shall drink, nor about your body, what you shall put on. Is not life more than food, and the body more than clothing? Look at the birds of the air: they neither sow nor reap nor gather into barns, and yet your heavenly Father feeds them. Are you not of more value than they?
>
> And which of you by being anxious can add one cubit to his span of life? And why are you anxious about clothing? Consider the lilies of the field, how they grow; they neither toil nor spin; yet I tell you, even Solomon in all his glory was not arrayed like one of these. But if God so clothes the grass of the field, which today is alive and tomorrow is thrown into the oven, will He not much more clothe you, O men of little faith?
>
> Therefore do not be anxious, saying, "What shall we eat?" or "What shall we drink?" or "What shall we wear?" For the Gentiles seek all these things; and your heavenly Father knows that you need them all. But seek first His kingdom and His righteousness, and all these things shall be yours as well (Matt. 6:25-33, RSV).

The word *anxiety* comes from the Latin root meaning "to strangle." At some time or other, all of us have had the experience of being strangled by anxiety, of having our peace of mind choked off by worry, of having our motivation and energy paralyzed by fear.

Psychologists tell us that there are two main sources of anxiety. One is any kind of *threat* to a personal value. We feel anxious when the safety of our children is threatened. We feel anxious when our reputation is threatened. We feel anxious when our financial security is threatened.

A second source of anxiety is *conflict*. The conflict can be experienced interpersonally or intrapersonally. An example of an intrapersonal conflict is what is called an *approach-approach* conflict. To *approach* is to have a tendency to do something, while to *avoid* is to resist doing something. In an approach-approach conflict, a person is faced with a situation in which he can't decide between two enticing opportunities. For example, a young man may have the opportunity of marrying the boss's daughter or the poor but beautiful girl next door.

The *approach-avoidance* conflict is one in which something is both desirable and undesirable. On the one hand, I would really like to be in peak physical condition; but on the other hand, I don't like to run and I love to eat unhealthy food. An *avoidance-avoidance* conflict is one in which both choices are undesirable. A high school student might be given the choice of cleaning his room or studying calculus, neither of which is particularly appealing. That's like asking a person if he would rather be audited by the IRS or have kidney stones.

Because life is full of threats to our values and conflicts between our values, there are plenty of opportunities for us to become anxious, to be paralyzed by worry, to be suffocated by indecision and apprehension. Yet there is an antidote to anxiety, the antidote of faith in God's sovereignty, goodness, and activity.

Jesus instructed His disciples not to be anxious, for God is *sovereign*. To be sovereign means that God is supreme, that He has total authority over every circumstance. It means that He knows our needs, our conflicts, the threats to our values, and He knows how to care for us in every situation. Faith in God's sovereignty will counteract anxiety.

We also need faith that God is *good*. Our God is eager for our needs to be met, for the threats to our values to be overcome, and for our conflicts to be resolved. He wants us to experience the best and nothing less.

Not only does God desire what is good for us, but He is *active* in taking the initiative to work for our good. We do not have a passive God who sits nonchalantly on the balcony of heaven watching our lives pass by. Our God is active, dynamic, industrious, and involved. Because He is *sovereign*, He knows our needs. Because He is *good*, He takes the initiative to actively meet our needs. As we put our faith in God and trust Him to be sovereign, good, and active in our lives, we will let go of our anxieties.

Activator of Positive Emotions

To activate something is to set in motion an energy which has been dormant. A wife might activate her dormant husband by promising to fix his favorite meal if he will wash the windows (or in the case of some wives, by promising to get her mother—or his—to cook his favorite meal). We activate our dormant cars by turning the ignition key and pressing on the accelerator.

Faith is the activator of our positive emotions. When we respond to God's truth by believing it and by acting on it, the natural result will be the growth of constructive, healthy emotions.

What emotions are activated by faith? Many of the people I interviewed said that their faith produces feelings of hopefulness and joy. Because of their faith in God, they know that there is always hope for the future, that good will ultimately triumph over evil, that justice will come to the oppressed, that sickness will someday be vanquished by health and wholeness. With faith in God, it is possible to experience His joy in every circumstance of life, to be eternally optimistic about the future.

Others have shared with me that their faith in God activates their motivation to work hard, that it releases untapped resources of energy. Their faith provides them a sense of purpose, a conviction that life is meaningful and worthwhile.

Have you ever found yourself feeling totally drained, completely exhausted by endless responsibilities and hassles? Have you ever felt as though you just couldn't drag yourself out of bed to face another day?

If so, then let faith activate your dormant energy and enthusiasm for life. Remind yourself of the liberating truth that you are a unique creation, a child of God, called and gifted by God to bring freshness to a stale world. Remind yourself that you have been called and equipped by God to sing the Gospel with your life and your lips to a world that has lost its song. Faith that believes and acts on the liberating truth of Scripture cannot help but activate such energy, strength, and enthusiasm.

I asked the people I interviewed: "When your faith in God is strong, how do you feel?" Here are some of their answers:

- "I feel forgiven."
- "I feel loved."
- "I feel courageous."
- "I feel relaxed."
- "I feel as free as a bird."
- "I feel bold."
- "I feel eager to live."
- "I feel at peace."
- "I feel hopeful."
- "I feel strong."

How are you feeling right now? Is your warehouse of emotions stored with more negative feelings than positive? Instead of feeling forgiven and loved and energetic, are you anxious and depressed?

If you're feeling negative, remember that it's OK to feel this way sometimes. God gave us our emotions and He can use all of them for our benefit. One writer put it this way:

> Take away my capacity for pain and you rob me of the possibility for joy. Take away my ability to fail and I would not know the meaning of success. Let me be immune to rejection and heartbreak and I could not know the glory of living (Ross W. Morris, *Leadership*, Winter 1982, Vol. III, No. 1, p. 58).

If you long to rid yourself of the pain negative emotions bring, there is an antidote. If you want to be free to laugh and to sing and to dance and to shout, there is something that can activate those feelings. The activator of your positive emotions is faith that believes and then acts on the truth of God. Take faith, and allow it to activate those powerfully positive emotions God has provided for your pleasure!

4 | Faith That Moves Mountains

I am fascinated by mountains. Because I grew up in Minnesota, the land of 10,000 lakes but nary a mountain, the only mountains I knew about as a preschooler were those I saw on television or in *National Geographic*. When I turned five, our family traveled to California to visit relatives. This meant that for the first time I would see mountains and the ocean. I could hardly wait!

My father told me that we wouldn't reach the mountains until we arrived in Colorado. But he made the mistake of saying that I would be able to see the mountains from some distance because of their size. So by the time we got to southern Minnesota, I started looking for the mountains. I was sure we would be able to see them from South Dakota, and I started to really get obnoxious about it in Nebraska. When we crossed the state line into Colorado and I still couldn't see any mountains, I began to think that my parents and older brother were playing a big joke on me and that the mountains were about as real as Santa Claus.

Finally my father spotted the snowcapped peaks or the

Rocky Mountains. At first I thought he was teasing me because they looked so much like the clouds I had often mistaken for mountains along the way. But mountains they were. We spent the next few days driving in and exploring the mountains of Colorado, and I thought I had reached heaven. We did some climbing, had a snowball fight, threw rocks over cliffs, went on a tour of a deep underground cavern, and collected pinecones. I dreamed about bears and stared at the towering peaks that looked to my five-year-old eyes like they reached into outer space. Ever since that trip I have had a love affair with mountains.

Yet while mountains are impressive to look at, they are also quite difficult to get around. As I drive through them, I often wonder what it must have been like for the pioneers who first settled our country to traverse the Rockies and the Sierra Nevadas of California without superhighways, without 200-horsepower engines, without maps showing the easiest and quickest route to take, without knowing what was on the other side of the mountain they were climbing.

The mountains of Israel don't compare in size with those of Colorado, Switzerland, or Tibet. Yet when Jesus referred to mountains in His teachings, His listeners would have formed a mental image quite similar to our own. "For truly I say to you, if you have faith as a mustard seed, you shall say to this mountain, 'Move from here to there,' and it shall move; and nothing shall be impossible to you" (Matt. 17:20).

William Barclay provides us with some necessary background in understanding what Jesus is communicating through this startling verse:

When Jesus spoke about *removing mountains* He was using a phrase which the Jews knew well. . . . To tear up, to uproot, to pulverize mountains were all regular phrases for removing difficulties. Jesus never meant this to be taken physically and literally. After all, the ordinary man seldom finds any necessity to remove a physical mountain. What He meant was: "If you have faith enough, all difficulties can be solved, and even the hardest task can be accomplished" (*The Gospel of Matthew*, Vol. 2, The Westminster Press, p. 167).

To the first-century Jew, a mountain was an obstacle, a symbolic barrier that prevented him from reaching some good thing that he very much wanted. The locusts or a bad drought were mountains in the way of having a good harvest. The Roman government was a mountain that impeded his experience of freedom and independence. Staggering taxes were a mountain that robbed him of what he thought was rightfully his. Blindness, lameness, or disease were mountains to the sick.

What is your mountain? What is the obstacle in your life that looms so large in your eyes, that towers above you like Mt. Ranier? What is it that blocks your experience of the abundant life, that obstructs your spiritual growth, that throttles your attempts to achieve your goals? Perhaps your mountain is some circumstance that seems so repressive, inhibiting, and impossible to change. Perhaps your mountain is your personality, your character, or habits that you have labored without success to alter.

Whatever your mountain may be—unemployment, a broken relationship, large debts, a bad habit, an unpleasant work situation—the good news from Jesus is that the mountain can be moved!

Just to emphasize His point, Jesus made the same statement again later on, after having cursed the fig tree so that it shriveled.

Truly I say to you, if you have faith, and do not doubt, you shall not only do what was done to the fig tree, but even if you say to this mountain, "Be taken up and cast into the sea," it shall happen. And everything you ask in prayer, believing, you shall receive (Matt. 21:21-22).

The promise of Jesus is clear—our mountains can be moved. And the prerequisite for moving the mountains is just as clear—it takes *faith*.

"All good enough," you say. "But I've heard that and read that before. *How* does faith move the mountain? That's what I'd like to know! And what specifically do *I* do?"

Fair enough. Let's examine the specifics of how faith moves the mountain. There are two aspects of mountain-moving faith. The faith that moves mountains is faith that imagines and risks.

Faith That Imagines

Mountain-moving faith begins in our minds and in our imaginations. It begins with what we think, with what we believe, with what we dream.

Let's suppose that the mountain which prohibits you from becoming the godly person God wants you to be, from experiencing the exuberance of the abundant life, and from achieving the goals you have set for yourself, is something within you. Your mountain is not your boss or an economic recession or the bars of a jail cell. Your mountain is you—whether it is your personal habits or a physical handicap or an emotional difficulty. But when your mountain is you, how does faith move the mountain?

The Bible tells us clearly that the task of moving the mountain, of removing the obstacle, begins in our *minds*: "For as he thinks within himself, so he is" (Prov. 23:7). Our lives are shaped by what we think, what we believe and imagine. Our characters are formed and our mountains are moved by what happens inside of our heads. Early in this century, William James said, "The greatest discovery of my generation is that human beings can alter their lives by altering their attitudes of mind." Another psychologist said, "There is a deep tendency in human nature to become precisely like that which you habitually imagine yourself to be" (Quoted by Norman Vincent Peale, *The Power of Positive Thinking*, Prentice-Hall, p. 157). And the Apostle Paul put it this way: "And do not be conformed to this world, but be transformed by the renewing of your mind" (Rom. 12:2).

When we are faced with a mountain, our natural tendency is to focus on the mountain. Whether our eyes are open or shut, the picture etched on the brain is the mountain. We concentrate on how big the mountain is, how impossible it would be to move, and how much unhappiness it has caused by depriving us of our desired goal.

But faith draws a different picture. Faith doesn't see what we are not; it sees what we will be. Faith doesn't concentrate on what we aren't enjoying, but on what we will enjoy. Faith doesn't cling to what we can't achieve but reaches for what we will accomplish. Faith sees the transformation and the achievement as having happened. The mountain has already been moved.

One of the best golfers in the history of the game was Ben Hogan. When asked the secret of his game, Hogan explained that before a golf tournament he would mentally rehearse each shot, imagining himself making the perfect shot for each hole. Before hitting the ball during the tournament, Hogan would again imagine himself swinging the club, striking the ball, and following through on a perfectly placed shot. Then he would step up to the ball and rely on his "muscle memory" to carry out the shot just as he had imagined it.

One of the most successful techniques psychologists have employed in treating people with phobias involves a person's imagination through *systematic desensitization*. For example, suppose a doctor was treating a person who had a fear of crowds. In his office, the doctor would ask that patient to close his eyes and gradually relax until he was totally at ease. Then he would have the person imagine himself talking comfortably and confidently with one other person. Gradually he would help the patient progress to the point of imagining himself getting along without anxiety in a crowd of 10,000. The fearful person would probably find that what he had imagined in the counselor's office he now could do in real life. His life would be changed by imagining himself as he wanted to be rather than as he was.

In a similar way, the Christian can move mountains. Perhaps your mountain is your quick temper, your impatience, your irritability. By faith make it a daily practice to imagine yourself as a gentle, patient, kind person. Remember, you become like your thoughts. You are drawn toward the picture you hold in your mind.

As the people of God, our faith is in more than a psychological process. Our faith is in the truth that God has promised to transform us into the image of Jesus Christ when we put our trust in His power. By faith you can confidently imagine the power of God being released in you to change you into a godly person, molding and shaping you into the person God wants you to be and that you want to be.

Perhaps you would like to be a bold, dynamic witness for Jesus Christ, but fear is the mountain that repulses your efforts. By faith in God's power to transform you, imagine yourself witnessing boldly, effectively, and without fear. Perhaps you have a project that you would like to complete, but the mountain of laziness or procrastination has you handcuffed. By faith you can move your mountain by seeing the project completed, by imagining yourself as a disciplined, dedicated, and determined person, energetically and passionately working to accomplish your dream.

The individuals who change our world are people with enough faith to envision possibilities and to dream of what could be. The greatest achievements of mankind begin as ideas which are then translated into reality after they are liberally fertilized with faith. In 1976 Steven Jobs had an idea and a dream. Beginning in a garage, the 21-year-old man began to work at his dream; in six years he had built Apple Computer into a multimillion-dollar corporation. St. Paul's Cathedral in London, the church that served as a symbol of hope to Londoners during the air raids of World War II, began as an idea, a mental image, a dream in the mind of the great architect Christopher Wren. Man's first walk on the moon had been imagined long before it happened on July 20, 1969. The faith that moves the mountain is the faith that imagines the mountain as already having been moved.

Faith That Risks!

Anytime we learn something new or change our character or make an impact on the life of another person, we do so only because we have been willing to take a risk. The person who has learned to ski has had to risk falling, being laughed at, getting cold and wet, and even getting hurt. Growth of any kind demands that we be willing to risk.

Do you recall the three servants in the Parable of the Talents in Matthew 25? One man was given five talents (about $5,000 in our money), one was given two talents, and the other was given one talent. The owner of the property who entrusted his wealth to these three men went away for a time, and when he returned he checked in with his servants to see how well they had managed his funds.

The owner learned that the first two employees had doubled what they were given. His response to each of them was, "Well done, good and faithful servant; you have been faithful over a little, I will set you over much; enter into the joy of your master" (v. 21, RSV). The third servant had done nothing to increase his talent, but had buried it in the ground for safekeeping. In anger, the owner took back the money and threw the servant out because of his worthlessness.

What should we learn from this parable? Jesus, as the owner, has entrusted His own wealth to each of us. He has equipped us with power and placed in our hands the treasure of the Gospel. He has bestowed abilities and potential which He expects to be used, not buried in the ground for safekeeping. Jesus calls us to invest the resources He has given us in order to grow spiritually and to minister to the world. But investing means taking a *risk*.

The owner in the parable condemned the third servant for his unwillingness to risk, and for hoarding his trust instead of investing it.

God has called us to invest our resources in order to multiply them, instead of encasing our God-given resources within the walls of church or home in order to preserve them. According to Jesus, the disciple who is full of faith is the one who risks.

If we want to make a positive impact on our society and our world, it is necessary for us to take risks. The Bible commands us to be actively involved in communicating the message of the Gospel to non-Christians. To do that requires that we develop relationships with non-Christians, and this may involve possible rejection or putting our reputation on the line as Jesus did. In developing a relationship with another person, we take the risk of having our foibles and our warts exposed, of being embarrassed or even humiliated. We may be let down, betrayed, or hurt. Relationships are a risky business.

That is where faith comes in. By faith we reach out in love to another person because we believe the risk of being rejected is outweighed by the value of a new relationship. By faith we force ourselves to risk falling on our faces because we believe the value of developing a new skill, changing our character or changing our world, is worth it.

Moving the mountain is impossible without the faith that risks. Faith is not passive. It begins with an intellectual belief but goes beyond that. Faith is active. Faith not only believes that the water is fine—it also jumps in. Faith not only believes the bridge is safe—it crosses over. Faith does not stand still, waiting for something to happen. Faith *makes* something happen.

In her book *Pathfinders*, Gail Sheehy identifies the qualities of people who are the movers and shakers of society and who experience the most satisfaction in their lives. She concludes that the most important quality of a pathfinder is the *willingness to risk*.

> One of the first things I discovered about pathfinders is that they are willing to risk change. They do not expect to cruise through life in a sports car along a well-marked superhighway. Confronted with an obstacle or an accident along the way, they try a detour that usually turns out to be constructive. . . . In my own studies, the people enjoying highest well-being were the most likely to describe having undergone a major change in their outlook values, personal affiliations, or career (William Morrow and Co., pp. 76-77).

By faith Moses risked picking up a snake and God transformed the snake into the very rod Moses later used to part the waters of the Red Sea. By faith Joshua risked besieging Jericho with horns, trumpets, and shouts, and the walls of the city crumbled so that Jericho was defeated. By faith Gideon risked attacking the Midianites, a people as numerous as "the sand which is upon the seashore" with only 300 men. The risk paid off when the Midianites in confusion battled each other so that they were easily defeated by Gideon's men. By faith David risked fighting the giant Goliath and defending the honor of Israel, using only a slingshot. The risk paid off when David's first toss found its mark and the Philistine army fled in fear.

Are there mountains that stand between you and your dreams? Are there mountains that stand between you and the spread of the Gospel? Are there mountains that stand between you and the abundant life?

Don Bennett conquered his mountain in July of 1982. For 10 years he had dreamed of climbing Mt. Rainier, the glacier-clad 14,400-foot mountain in the state of Washington. On Sunday, July 18th at 9:00 A.M., Don Bennett reached the summit, a remarkable achievement for a 52-year-old.

Yet Don Bennett had a more important reason for climbing Mt. Rainier than just because it was there. On behalf of the National Handicapped Sports and Recreation Association, he wanted to publicize what handicapped people can do, giving hope to others who are handicapped. Don Bennett *hopped* to the top of Mt. Rainier on one leg. He lost the other leg in a boating accident in 1972. Don Bennett took a risk, he acted on his dream, and he conquered his mountain.

Jesus Christ told His followers 2,000 years ago, "If you have faith as a mustard seed, you shall say to this mountain, 'Move from here to there,' and it shall move; and nothing shall be impossible to you." As Christians we have been called and equipped by God to do the impossible. We have been called and equipped by God to transform our world.

But it takes faith that can imagine, and visualize the mountain as having already been moved. It takes faith that acts, faith that risks, faith that tries. It takes faith that believes God will do what He has promised to do.

Whatever your mountain may be, take faith—you can move it!

5 Faith That Doesn't Quit

I am a very competitive person and I don't like to lose. While I have become a much more gracious loser with the passing of time, I still find that losing any kind of game—racquetball, Uno, or Pac-Man—can ruin my whole day. Unless I happen to be feeling especially mature that day, losing can leave me grumpy and withdrawn.

It is especially painful to lose to my wife. While I love and cherish Brenda more than anyone else in the world, I have discovered something inside of me that compels me to compete with her. Fortunately for my ego, I am still able to beat her in racquetball. But I have never been able to beat her in video games. For me to compete against Brenda in a video game is like trying to compete against Mario Andretti in the Indianapolis 500, driving a Volkswagen. No matter how much I practice, Brenda can pick up a new game and beat me at it on her first try.

You can imagine how hard it is for a highly competitive, stubborn, proud, 20th-century American male like myself to lose to his wife. Fortunately, Brenda does not gloat; but just the same, I am steaming inside when I lose. I feel like one large exposed nerve every time I lose another game of Space Invaders or Pac-Man to her.

In fact, it is so painful for me to lose to my wife that I have resorted to a tactic that I often used when I was growing up. It's a sure-fire way for a person who hates to lose to maintain some semblance of dignity in the face of certain defeat. When we're in the middle of a game that I'm sure to lose, I quit. I'll stop playing and graciously say, "Honey, I'm tired of playing. I think I'll go read for a while." At which time I will go off into the corner to pout and pretend to read the newspaper until Brenda finishes the game and comes over to cheer me up with a hug and a kiss.

Have you ever used that tactic? Have you ever quit when you were losing a race? Have you ever felt like walking out of your job, or giving up on your marriage or on a child who hasn't turned out the way you hoped he would? Or have you ever been tempted to stop trusting God, to give up on Him when your prayers seemed to go unanswered, when your pain is unrelieved, and your dreams have crumbled into dust with the passing of the years?

We are all goaded by life's thorns and bruises into wanting to give up on something, to quit, to resign, to check out. Sometimes the pressures from our environment and the tensions from inside build to such a point that the only thing our panicked minds can see is to bail out. Victor Frankl, in writing about his experience at the death camps of Auschwitz and Dachau during World War II, explained how many of his compatriots became so worn down physically and so depleted emotionally by the day-to-day tyranny of their captors that they finally just gave up and died.

It takes faith to keep on trying, trusting, and obeying God when the only reward of obedience seems to be trouble. Yes, to move the mountain that impedes your experience of abundant life requires faith. But to keep on believing and to wait patiently—even when God rules that the mountain must not be moved—requires a special kind of faith.

As much as I admire and try to emulate people who have moved mountains, I think I admire even more those people of faith who have endured when the mountain wouldn't budge, or when it came crashing down on top of them. Such people have refused to quit, even when everything seemed to be working against them.

Dr. Widen is one of them. He was a doctor to my grandparents, my parents, and my brothers and me. He was widely know for his prowess as a tennis player, and as a man with a deep faith in God. After his love for God, Dr. Widen reserved his greatest love for his wife. His love for her didn't waver one bit when she suffered a series of strokes and became paralyzed.

Because she needed round-the-clock attention he couldn't provide while he maintained his practice, Dr. Widen found it necessary to have his wife cared for in a nursing home. He rented an apartment near the hospital he served in Minneapolis, but used it strictly for sleeping. His leisure hours were spent with his wife.

Every day after work, Dr. Widen would drive to the nursing home across town to feed his wife and to tell her about his day. She had lost her speech and could respond to his comments only with a slight squeeze of the hand and the hint of a smile. Those who knew Dr. Widen well said that he lived to see his wife smile. That made it all worthwhile for him. That and his faith in God, for his faith wasn't shattered when his wife's ill health didn't improve, despite his fervent prayers.

When Dr. Widen finally retired, after traveling to be with his wife each evening for over 10 years, he moved into the nursing home. When she died recently, she died knowing that she was loved by a husband who was faithful to her in sickness as well as in health. Dr. Widen refused to give up on his wife or on God.

To be strong in faith means to be faithful. It is interesting to note that the same Greek word is used for *faith* and for *faithfulness*. When we read in Ephesians 2:8 that we are saved by grace through faith, the Greek word for "faith" is *pistos*. In Revelation 19:11, Jesus Christ is described as the one who is faithful and true, and again the word for "faithful" is the Greek word *pistos*. The appropriate translation depends on the context.

A person of faith is faithful. To be faithful is to be loyal and reliable. To be faithful is to persevere and endure. To be faithful means that you don't quit.

One of the primary themes of the Book of Revelation is faithfulness. The book is both prophetic and pastoral. As a prophet, John wrote to inform his readers that ultimately the wicked would be judged and the righteous vindicated. As a pastor, he wrote to give comfort and encouragement to a suffering church, and most of all to challenge Christians to be faithful.

Often we think of Revelation as a book whose primary function is to tell us what's going to happen in the future. Yet notice the blessing that is promised in Revelation 1:3: "Blessed is he who reads and those who hear the words of the prophecy, and heed the things which are in it; for the time is near."

The same promise is repeated at the end of the book: "Blessed is he who heeds the words of the prophecy of this book" (22:7).

Revelation is not a book to be read just for information and insight. It is a book to be obeyed. And the primary command, running through every chapter, is this: "Be faithful! Endure! Don't give up! Don't quit!"

To discover exactly what it means to be faithful, let's look briefly at the letters to the seven churches, found in Revelation 2 and 3.

Be Faithful to Death

In Revelation 2:8-11 we read the letter to the church at Smyrna:

> And to the angel of the church in Smyrna write: The first and the last, who was dead, and has come to life, says this: "I know your tribulation and your poverty (but you are rich), and the blasphemy by those who say they are Jews and are not, but are a synagogue of Satan. Do not fear what you are about to suffer. Behold, the devil is about to cast some of you into prison, that you may be tested, and you will have tribulation ten days. Be faithful until death, and I will give you the crown of life. He who has an ear, let him hear what the Spirit says to the churches. He who overcomes shall not be hurt by the second death."

Revelation was written by the Apostle John, most likely during the reign of the Emperor Domitian, who ruled the Roman Empire A.D. 81—96. John had been exiled to the penal colony on the Isle of Patmos for his preaching and ministry, and so he wrote Revelation to the suffering church as one who was well acquainted with suffering.

Smyrna was a proud and beautiful city located 35 miles north of Ephesus on the west shore of the Aegean Sea. Smyrna had close ties with Rome and strongly encouraged its citizens to offer worship to the Roman emperor. Smyrna also had a very large Jewish population which was known for its antipathy toward Christians. Robert Mounce notes, "This strong allegiance to Rome, plus a large Jewish population which was actively hostile to the Christians, made it exceptionally difficult to live as a Christian in Smyrna" ("The

Book of Revelation," *New International Commentary on the New Testament,* Eerdmans, p. 91).

What did faithfulness mean to the Christians in Smyrna? It meant being obedient and loyal to Jesus Christ even if that faithfulness resulted in death—and for many of them it did. Jesus' message to this church made no bones about the fact that they were going to suffer. The original readers of the letter knew exactly what Jesus meant when He said that some of them would be thrown into prison. In their world, prison was a place to await execution. Polycarp, the well-known church father from Smyrna, provided an example of faithfulness to his church members. When he refused to worship Caesar as Lord, Polycarp was tied to a funeral pyre and burned to death. Many others also were "faithful until death" and were executed by the Roman government.

Faithfulness to Jesus Christ means not quitting, not giving up. It means to keep obeying even if the reward of obedience is death. It means to be loyal, to be willing to endure any consequence for the sake of what you believe.

While traveling in Europe, my wife and I stopped to explore the catacombs near the ancient city of Rome. After winding our way through a few of the many miles of catacombs, we emerged from underground into the Basilica of St. Sebastian.

Sebastian was a high-ranking military officer during the reign of Domitian, and a close friend of the emperor. Unknown to Domitian, Sebastian was also a Christian. He kept that fact hidden from Domitian and from his colleagues so that he would be free to sneak supplies and give encouragement to the Christians in jail. It was a risky venture, but for quite some time Sebastian's efforts went undetected.

But finally Sebastian was found out. Being a friend of Domitian didn't help Sebastian a bit. He was sentenced to death and shot with arrows.

Curiously, though, Sebastian didn't die from the arrows. The soldiers assumed him to be dead; but a woman named Irene, whose husband had been executed for his faith, found Sebastian alive, removed the arrows, and nursed him back to health.

Sebastian was not through. He believed that God had spared his life so that he could explain the Gospel to Domitian. What a difference it would make if the Roman emperor himself were to be converted! It would mean an end to the slaughter, and freedom for his brothers and sisters. In faithfulness to what he believed God had called him to do, Sebastian, who knew Domitian's favorite places for his evening walk, found the emperor alone, and with conviction and enthusiasm explained the good news about Jesus Christ.

Domitian was unmoved. For a second time he ordered that his friend be executed. To insure that Sebastian died, death was to be by clubbing. This time the executioners completed their task. Sebastian's faithfulness cost him his life.

The church at Pergamum had martyrs as well. In their letter we read, "I know where you dwell, where Satan's throne is; and you hold fast My name, and did not deny My faith, even in the days of Antipas, My witness, My faithful one, who was killed among you, where Satan dwells" (Rev. 2:13).

Legend has it that Antipas was put to death during Domitian's reign by being slowly roasted in a brazen bull. Commentators point out that the most significant thing about Antipas is that he was a faithful witness. That phrase is important because it is the same title Jesus was given: "And from Jesus Christ, the faithful witness, the firstborn of the dead, and the ruler of the kings of the earth" (Rev. 1:5).

The Greek word for "witness" is *martus*, from which we get our word *martyr*. A martyr is someone who is put to death for his faith. Antipas was obedient to the command to be faithful until death. His unwillingness to quit and his commitment to endure resulted in his martyrdom.

The readers of Revelation were encouraged as they remembered that Jesus, who called them to be faithful until death, had gone before them. Jesus had set the example. He was the first faithful witness, the first faithful martyr.

Be Faithful Without Compromise

For most Christians living in North America in the 20th century, faithfulness to Jesus Christ will not result in martyrdom. Yet living faithfully is just as difficult as dying for faith. The church at Thyatira was challenged to show its faithfulness to Jesus, not by dying but by living uncompromising and godly lives in a pagan environment (Rev. 2:18-29).

Thyatira was distinguished in the ancient world for its large number of trade guilds. A guild was roughly equivalent to a union. Because the trade guilds were intimately related to the local religions, they posed a special threat to the economic well-being of Christians. To be admitted to a guild, a person had to pledge loyalty to the local gods. At the very least, he had to be willing to participate in a common meal dedicated to a pagan deity. Exclusion from the guild meant economic disaster.

In the message to the church at Thyatira, there is mention of a woman named Jezebel who had led the Christians into immorality. Most commentators reason that Jezebel was a Christian woman from the church at Thyatira. They suggest that she led the church astray by teaching that it was acceptable for Christians to accommodate themselves to the pagan religious practices in order to gain entrance into the trade guilds: "After all, the idols they worship aren't real anyway, and God wouldn't want His people to starve when they didn't have to, would He?"

The name of the game for Jezebel was *compromise*. What harm could there be in eating a meal in honor of gods that didn't exist? But as usually happens, a little compromise led to a bigger one. First it was eating a meal, then it was being sexually involved with the temple prostitutes.

To be faithful to Jesus Christ means to be unwilling to compromise on the essentials of faith and practice. Faithfulness means unwillingness to alter records to save some money on our income tax. It means refusing to give lustful thoughts room and board, even if just for the night. Faithfulness means being stubbornly loyal to our values and our beliefs. It means taking a stand for what we believe is right, even if that results in losing a business deal, not getting a promotion, or even losing a job.

To exhibit the faith that doesn't quit is to be faithful to our moral standards, no matter what the economic cost. To the church at Thyatira, to you and to me, Jesus says, "Be faithful without compromise."

Be Faithful When You're Tired

Faithfulness is especially hard when you're tired. Whether it's a physical or emotional weariness, exhaustion can easily lead the faithful away from faithfulness. The church at Sardis was a perfect example of that. Listen to what Jesus had to say to the Christians there.

> I know your deeds, that you have a name that you are alive, and you are dead. Wake up, and strengthen the things that remain, which were about to die; for I have not found your deeds completed in the sight of My God.
> Remember therefore what you have received and heard; and keep it, and repent. If therefore you will not wake up, I will come like a thief, and you will not know at what hour I will come upon you (Rev. 3:1-3).

The church at Sardis should have been alive and flourishing. From all that we know about Sardis, the church was relatively free of internal heresy and external opposition.

But instead of being alive, they were dead. In the absence of opposition, they had become complacent. Their faith had atrophied from lack of use. They grew weary, and finally fell comfortably to sleep.

The words of Jesus to the church at Sardis would have struck a tender nerve in people who knew the history of their city. Sardis was built on top of a steep hill. The cliffs surrounding Sardis towered 1,500 feet above the valley below. Because of its setting, Sardis was virtually inaccessible to invading armies. The people of the city slept securely at night, even when their enemies sat watching them from the valley below.

But twice in her history, Sardis had been attacked. The first time was when Cyrus invaded the city in 549 B.C. For days his troops were easily beaten back by the soldiers of Sardis. In frustration Cyrus promised a promotion to any soldier able to plan a successful raid on the city. One night one of his men was watching a guard who stood at the top of the cliff. The guard clumsily dropped his helmet down the cliff. Thinking he was unwatched, he climbed down the cliff to retrieve his helmet and then climbed back up to his post. The enemy soldier watched his descent and ascent carefully and memorized the path he took.

The next night Cyrus sent a few men up the side of the cliff led by the soldier who had memorized the way. When they reached the top, they discovered all of the guards asleep! They made their way to the city gate, opened the gate to let in their comrades, and sacked the sleeping city of Sardis.

To be caught napping once is bad enough, but Sardis was caught twice. In 216 B.C., Antiochus the Great used the same tactic as Cyrus had. On reaching the wall of the city, he found the guards asleep and captured Sardis.

It was to the church in the sleeping city of Sardis that Jesus proclaimed, "Wake up! ... If therefore you will not wake up, I will come like a thief, and you will not know at what hour I will come upon you."

What caused the Christians at Sardis to fall asleep spiritually? Perhaps they had become too secure, too safe, too comfortable. Perhaps they had stopped growing, stopped stretching their faith. Maybe their faith seemed to no longer have relevance to them.

Whatever the cause, Jesus' inspection of the church revealed that they were sound asleep. They were spiritually out for the count. "For I have not found your deeds completed in the sight of My God." The Christians at Sardis had fallen asleep on their shovels before they had finished digging the hole.

Faithfulness to Jesus Christ means to finish what we've started, even when our eyelids are droopy and our legs feel like lead. Faithfulness means following through on our commitments. It means keeping active in our task of taking the Gospel to the world, and not giving up until every person in our community has heard the news that he is loved by Jesus Christ.

Unfaithfulness means to quit growing spiritually, to quit studying God's Word, to quit worshiping with the people of God, to quit praying, to quit singing God's praises and proclaiming His love.

To people who are too secure in their faith, and to others who are weary from doing good, Jesus says, "Be faithful! Complete what you've begun! Don't quit!"

Be Faithful in Ministry
The last of the seven letters is to the church at Laodicea. It begins with these words:

The Amen, the faithful and true Witness, the Beginning of the creation of God, says this: "I know your deeds, that you are neither cold nor hot; I would that you were cold or hot. So because you are lukewarm, and neither hot nor cold, I will spit you out of My mouth" (Rev. 3:14-16).

Because Laodicea had an inadequate water supply, most of its water had to be piped in. Six miles north of Laodicea was Hierapolis, a city famous for hot springs used for medicinal purposes. To the south was the city of Colossae which had its own water source. Its water was cold, and good for drinking.

When Jesus called the Laodicean church "lukewarm," He was not referring to the spiritual temperature of the church. He was rather chastising them for their unfaithfulness in ministry. The church in Laodicea was neither cold, meaning it was not providing refreshment for the spiritually weary, nor hot, meaning that it was not providing healing for the spiritually sick.

What's more refreshing than a drink of cold water or a cool shower on a warm, muggy day? What's more healing for weary muscles than a hot mineral whirlpool? The church at Laodicea was neither cold nor hot. They provided neither refreshment nor healing. Their unfaithfulness was in their ministry. To be faithful in ministry means to keep ministering to people till we've met their needs, refreshed the weary, and healed the broken. James put it this way:

If a brother or sister is without clothing and in need of daily food, and one of you says to them, "Go in peace, be warmed and be filled," and yet you do not give them what is necessary for their body, what use is that? (James 2:15-16)

When the Samaritan saw a man beaten, stripped naked, and robbed, lying by the side of the road, he couldn't help but stop. And he didn't stop helping until he had met the man's need. He poured oil and wine on his wounds to heal him. He bandaged his bruises and cuts. He transported him to an inn, and paid for his lodging and care. The Samaritan didn't stop until he was assured that he had done all he could to be an agent of refreshment and healing to a broken, abandoned stranger. That is faithfulness.

There are times when our bodies and our spirits call out to us to quit. Or the tedium of a job urges us to quit. The struggle of making a marriage work, when the pressures of finances and unmet expectations close in on us, suggests that we cash in the relationship and hope for a better one next time.

The apparent silence of God in the face of our constant prayers for relief from our pain, for respite from our grief, for healing for our disease, provides us with all the incentive we need to give up on God, to quit trusting and obeying Him.

But faith doesn't quit. It waits. It perseveres. It doesn't give up, no matter what the odds are. Sometimes it requires gritting our teeth and clenching our fists. Sometimes it means praying the same prayer for the same person for the thousandth time. Sometimes it means sacrifice, tears, and may even mean death. Regardless of the cost, faith doesn't quit.

If you feel that you can't possibly go on, that you are extended beyond your limit, or that time has run out on you, then take faith—in the God who never gives up on you. Take faith in the God who always comes through right on schedule—His schedule. Take faith in the God who paved the way for you through His Son Jesus. Take faith in the truth that life is meaningful, that your efforts are not in vain (1 Cor. 15:58). Take faith in the truth that there is always hope, that at the heart of the universe there is joy, and that heaven is ahead of us.

By God's grace you can endure! Take faith—the faith that never quits!

6 | Faith That Refreshes

What recharges your batteries? Where do you turn when your body and soul need refreshing, when your spirit needs reviving, and your love for life needs rekindling?

When I think of refreshment, the first image that comes to my mind is water. When I'm hot and thirsty, there's nothing like a drink of ice water and a cool shower to rejuvenate my tired body. When my nerves are frayed at the edges and my motivation level is a quart or two low, there's nothing as soothing as sitting on the beach listening to the ocean hissing, rumbling, and throbbing, and watching the waves swelling and cresting before they come tumbling toward shore. And when my muscles are sore and my head aches, there's nothing like lounging in a jacuzzi, enveloped by hot, swirling water, to relax my body and to reactivate my sagging spirit.

What refreshes you? For some people, eating a new flavor of ice cream is refreshing. Others are refreshed by a back-rub, by getting a letter from an old friend, or by taking a day off to do nothing. For many of us, music is refreshing.

To be refreshed is to be renewed. It is to be given a clearer perspective, to be energized by a newfound source of strength. When I asked people to describe for me how they would describe a person of faith, the word *refreshing* popped up over and over again.

There is something about a person of faith that is enlivening, that reminds us to smile, that restores the twinkle in our eyes. There is something about a person of faith that smooths our wrinkled brows and straightens our shoulders.

Perhaps the most refreshing personality in the New Testament, other than our Lord, is Philemon. The book bearing his name is one of the shortest in the New Testament, and is sandwiched between Titus and Hebrews. Paul wrote this brief letter to Philemon from a prison in Rome around A.D. 60.

The letter is an appeal by Paul for Philemon to show mercy to his runaway slave, Onesimus. From the letter we learn that Onesimus had fled to Rome, where he was converted through Paul's ministry (v. 10). Paul was now sending Onesimus back bearing this letter, to encourage Philemon to welcome Onesimus, not just as a repentant slave, but as a new brother in Christ (v. 16).

It is in verses 4-7 of Philemon that we learn what kind of person Philemon was and the quality of faith he demonstrated:

I thank my God always when I remember you in my prayers, because I hear of your love and of the faith which you have toward the Lord Jesus and all the saints, and I pray that the sharing of your faith may promote the knowledge of all the good that is ours in Christ. For I have derived much joy and comfort from your love, my brother, because the hearts of the saints have been refreshed through you (RSV).

Let's take a closer look at these verses to discover just how Philemon's faith enabled him to refresh the hearts of the saints.

Faith That Loves and Believes in Jesus Christ

From verse 5 we learn that Philemon was known for his love for Jesus Christ and for his faith in Christ. Philemon had a reputation, according to Paul, for being totally and unreservedly committed to Jesus. Now most people might think that to become a refreshing, enlivening, energetic person, the first thing would be to enroll in a course on "How to Win Friends and Influence People." For the most important ingredient of a refreshing personality, they might choose a quick-witted sense of humor, or good breeding, or suavity, or charisma.

But in truth, the first and most important ingredient of a truly refreshing person is a total commitment to Jesus Christ. A refreshing person is one who loves and believes in Jesus Christ.

Have you ever known someone whose deep love for God can light up a whole room? Such a person is highly contagious. You can't help but catch his enthusiasm, vitality, and energy.

I am very grateful to God for the many refreshing people He has sent into my life, and just at those times when I most needed refreshing. During my first three years in San Jose, I served as assistant to Pastor Bernie Travaille, who retired in 1982 after 42 years of being a senior pastor. As his assistant, I had the opportunity to observe him closely and to see his faith in action on Monday evenings as well as on Sunday mornings. While I heard Pastor Travaille preach many inspiring sermons, the most vivid images that will always linger in my mind are of him singing congregational hymns and listening to the choir sing. I've never seen anyone enjoy singing hymns or listening to choral anthems more than Pastor Travaille. His face would beam, his eyes would sparkle, and his voice would resonate with elation whenever he had the opportunity to sing the praises of his Lord.

Do you remember how you were when you first fell in love? Do you remember how you walked with a bounce, how you always had a silly grin on your face, how you seemed to enjoy the food you ate and the work you did a little bit more than usual? While you probably weren't too aware of much else than that special person who occupied your thoughts so completely, your energy was infectious. For people who had started to take their own significant others for granted, your excitement and unashamed enthusiasm were refreshing!

That's how it is when we meet a person who is very much in love with God. When our spiritual fuel gauge is near empty, and our ambition to worship and serve God has been squashed flat like a tube of toothpaste in the hands of a two-year-old, it's refreshing to come into contact with a person excited about his relationship with Jesus Christ.

Jesus gave us a clue as to how this works. While in Jerusalem for the Feast of Tabernacles held annually near the end of September, Jesus took the opportunity to make a few statements to the crowds.

Now on the last day, the great day of the feast, Jesus stood and cried out, saying, "If any man is thirsty, let him come to Me and drink. He who believes in Me, as the Scripture said, 'From his innermost being shall flow rivers of living water.' " But this He spoke of the Spirit, whom those who believed in Him were to receive (John 7:37-39).

Within the person who believes in Jesus is a river of living water, a reservoir of power and strength ready to be released on command, flowing out to refresh and renew everyone around him. Within such an individual is the refreshing presence of the Holy Spirit, waiting to be poured out as a revitalizing stream.

The person who is filled with the Spirit of God, who is in love with God, who has made Jesus his Lord, is refreshing. The presence of the Holy Spirit residing within him is released to renew and resurrect the sapped spirits of weary and broken people.

Faith That Loves and Believes in People

As well as loving and believing in God, Philemon also had a reputation for loving and believing in people. Notice again what Paul had to say: "I thank my God always when I remember you in my prayers, because I hear of your love and of the faith which you have toward the Lord Jesus and all the saints" (vv. 4-5, RSV).

It is refreshing to be around someone who loves us and believes in us just the way we are. Too few people treat others as valuable, unique individuals worthy of respect. Angry drivers shake their fists at us for driving too slow or too fast. As students we've all been "blessed" with at least one professor who must have written his doctoral dissertation on "Fifty Ways to Publicly Humiliate Students." And we've all been to restaurants where waiters and waitresses have the gift of making us feel guilty for ordering a meal.

How refreshing to meet someone who loves you and believes in you just because you're you, who thinks you're terrific no matter how many freckles you have or how long your nose is. What a thrill it is to be treated as special!

While I was in seminary studying preaching, I received some advice from my mentor, Dan Erwin. He said, "Don't spend your energy telling people what's wrong with them. Don't concentrate on telling people what they aren't, what they haven't done. Instead, work hard at helping people visualized *what they can be* by the power of God. We already know what's wrong with us. We need people to help us see what we can be." That's how a person of faith refreshes others.

One of the most captivating speakers I know of is Dr. Howard Hendricks of Dallas Theological Seminary. On a tape about motivation, he tells what life was like for him while he was growing up. He says, "I can count on the fingers of one hand the number of people who saw me as anything other than a problem."

Then Dr. Hendricks tells about the only two school teachers he remembers, his fifth-grade teacher and his sixth-grade teacher. He recalls that his fifth-grade teacher struck terror into the hearts of students. She and Howard, who struck terror into the hearts of teachers, didn't get along too famously. Once, in desperation, she tied Howie to his chair with his hands behind his back and said, "There. Now sit still and behave."

When they graduated Howie to the sixth grade, he met his new teacher, who was 6'4" and "a female Sherlock Holmes." Her first words to him were, "Oh, so you're Howard Hendricks. I've heard about you." Then, as Howie took a big gulp, she continued, "But I want you to know that I don't believe a word of it."

That teacher, says Hendricks, was the first person who ever believed in him; and he resolved then and there never to let her down. His most vivid memory of sixth grade was of working furiously at his desk and then glancing up at the little window in the door at the open-mouthed face of his fifth-grade teacher who had to see this thing which had come to pass.

People who believe in us are refreshing. They invigorate and motivate us. They light the flame that we thought had been snuffed out by disappointment and frustration. By their faith in us they heal our wounds, they mend our brokenness, and set us free to start life over again. Their faith provides the spiritual springboard we needed to bounce back. It has been said, "Many people have gone further than they thought they could because someone else thought they could." By their faith in us, people of faith enable us to do and be more than we ever dreamed possible.

Two of the most famous sculptures in the world are the *Pieta* and the *David*, both by Michelangelo. The *Pieta*, in St. Peter's Cathedral in the Vatican, was done by Michelangelo when he was only 24. The hands, the muscles, the facial contours of the sculptures are so authentic that the pieces seem as alive as the people admiring them.

What makes these pieces even more remarkable is that each of them was carved out of a single piece of marble. To sculpt a perfectly proportioned human body out of a single piece of marble leaves no room for error. When asked the secret of his sculpting, Michelangelo explained that it was in what he saw in his mind's eye. When he would look at a freshly hewn hunk of marble, he would see the image of the piece he planned to sculpt. In his imagination, the figures he planned to sculpt were real people trapped in the marble, and it was his job to free them for the world to admire, by simply chipping away all the marble that was unnecessary.

A person of faith sees not just what people are, but what they can be. The person of faith looks past the rough edges that need to be chipped off and sees the beauty of the final product. The person of faith calls out the best in us by believing in us and helping us to see ourselves through his believing eyes.

When Paul and Barnabas were preparing to embark on their second missionary journey, Barnabas tried to convince Paul to take John Mark with them. Paul, remembering that

Mark had dropped out of the first tour, refused to let him come. But Barnabas saw more in Mark than his failure. Barnabas, whose name means "son of encouragement," believed in Mark so much that he was willing to separate from Paul and go with Mark. What was the result of Barnabas' faith in Mark? The earliest Gospel, which became the model for Matthew and Luke, was written by none other than John Mark.

The person who loves us as we are, and who has faith in what we can become by the power of God, is refreshing. Let's remember to be thankful for those people in our lives who by their love and their faith in us have refreshed us and called out the best in us. Thank God for Philemons!

Faith That Shares Good News

The third quality of a refreshing person, is found in verse 6 of Philemon: "And I pray that the sharing of your faith may promote the knowledge of all the good that is ours in Christ" (RSV).

Philemon's faith was shared. And I'm confident that Philemon did just what Paul prayed he would do—promote the knowledge of all the good that is ours in Christ. A refreshing person isn't a prophet of doom who spends his days conveying bad tidings. Rather, he shares the good news of all the wealth that we as Christians already possess.

My all-time favorite film is *The Wizard of Oz*. I have seen it, at last count, 17 times and can sing just about every song in the movie by heart (much to my wife's annoyance). At first I enjoyed the movie because I had a crush on Dorothy. When I got to be eight years old, I outgrew Dorothy and watched the show to see Toto, Dorothy's dog. Only in adult years did I see the message behind the entertainment. You may recall what Dorothy, the Scarecrow, the Tin Man, and the Cowardly Lion learned at the climax of their adventures in Oz. The Scarecrow had been distressed that he didn't have a brain, but the Wizard pointed out to him that he had as many brains as any person in a university. While the Wizard of Oz gave him a degree to confirm that fact, the truth was that the Scarecrow had had a brain all along. The Tin Man was in search of a heart, yet we knew all along that he already had a heart—how else could he shed tears. To the Cowardly Lion who was searching for courage, the Wizard of Oz pointed out that he had acted courageously in risking his life to help Dorothy.

Even Dorothy had what she had been looking for during the entire journey—a way home. She just didn't realize it! It took the Good Witch of the North to inform her that the ruby slippers she had been wearing could take her home, if she used them properly. Throughout their adventures, the four main characters of *The Wizard of Oz* already had exactly what they wanted and needed, but didn't know it. It just took a few words from the Wizard of Oz and the Good Witch to clue them in.

The person of faith is the one who comes along to clue us in to what we already have as Christians. He reminds us that everything we need and want is already available to us, in our possession. In Christ we are loved. In Christ we are forgiven. In Christ we have a family, a people to whom we belong. In Christ we have peace of mind, freedom from the fear of death, freedom from anxiety and guilt. In Christ we have power to remove mountains. We have joy and the power of self-control. In Christ we have security, a future to look forward to, a hope to celebrate. In Christ we have everything we need or could ever want. How refreshing it is—when we get our noses so buried in the dust of life—to have someone come along and remind us of who we are and what we have as children of our heavenly Father!

The refreshing person is the one who shares his faith by

communicating good news to people. Have you ever had the experience of being picked up, of being rejuvenated, by getting some good news? Perhaps it was a letter of acceptance from a school you wanted to attend. Maybe it was the news that a relative who had been seriously injured in an accident was recovering. Maybe you've been fortunate enough to receive the good news that you have won a contest and are going to receive a large sum of money. Good news can transform a frazzled and fatigued person into someone who can't keep a straight face.

There is no better news to be found anywhere than what the person of faith has to share—that Jesus Christ died to forgive our sins and to make it possible to personally relate to the God who created heaven and earth. That it's never too late to start over, that there's always hope for tomorrow. That Jesus not only died for us, but was resurrected, and that because He lives we can live too!

The person of faith knows that there is always good news behind the bad news. Some would accuse him of being unrealistic, of looking at life through rose-colored glasses. The person of faith never seems to notice how bad some people can be. He never seems to be agitated that there's another crisis in our government. The person of faith always seems to be talking about what's good, what's positive, what's hopeful.

To hear the good news the person of faith has to share is as refreshing as a mountain stream on a hot day. His faith washes over us and cleans away all the dirt and discouragement and cynicism that has weighed us down.

You too can be a refreshing person. You can give hope and encouragement to people who have forgotten how to smile. You can restore broken hearts, mend broken relationships, and revive broken dreams. How? By taking faith—the faith that refreshes!

7 How Much Faith Is Enough?

While I was in college the brother of a friend of mine developed a brain tumor. Immediately our Christian group at the University of Minnesota gathered to pray for his healing. As the weeks went by, however, Bill got worse rather than better. My friend became increasingly distraught as she saw her younger brother growing weaker and weaker; the rest of us did our best to pray more intensely and with more faith in God's healing power.

Finally, despite the best efforts of the medical profession, our zealous prayers, and the dedicated love of his family, Bill died. Even though we knew that he was better off in the presence of God, we were all heartbroken by his death and by the seeming futility of our prayers. Shortly after his death, with our frustration level still high and our emotions frayed, a member of our group made a statement to Bill's sister that she wished later she could retract: "If only you had had more faith, your brother wouldn't have died."

That statement smacked me between the eyes like a stone flung from a slingshot. My first reaction was, "Let's all get out of here before anyone else says something they don't mean." But as I mentally rehashed that uncomfortable moment, I began to wonder all over again about the role of faith in our prayers. Was it possible that Bill would have been healed if only his sister or his parents or the rest of us had had more faith? After all, didn't Jesus say, "And whatever you ask in prayer, you will receive, if you have faith"? (Matt. 21:22, RSV)

Yet, I thought, if ever there was anyone who had faith that God was going to do a miracle, it was Bill's sister. And while our group may not have been the most mature Christians in the world, when we prayed for Bill our faith in God seemed to us to be unshakable. Just how much faith is necessary before God will answer our prayers? How much faith is enough?

Years later I was reading Joni Eareckson's book *A Step Further* and noticed that she wondered about the same questions. She related in her book how she and the elders of her church prayed for her healing from paralysis, and how her questions multiplied as time passed and it became apparent that she wasn't being healed. In Joni's words:

> But then came to my mind the $10,000 question, the question that is in the minds of so many I've met over the years who have not been healed in response to their prayers—did I have enough faith?
>
> What a flood of guilt that question brings. It constantly leaves the door open for the despairing thought: God didn't heal me because there is something wrong with me. I must not have believed hard enough (Joni Eareckson and Steve Estes, Zondervan, p. 125).

Have you ever asked yourself, "How much faith is enough? How much faith does it take before God will hear my prayers?" Or have you ever allowed yourself to wonder if maybe the reason your family member wasn't healed was that you didn't have enough faith? Or have you ever had it suggested to you by a well-meaning friend that the reason your mountain hasn't moved is your little faith?

Most Christians wonder about those questions at some point in their lives for they are logical and natural questions. When the disciples were unable to cast a demon out of a young boy and asked Jesus for an explanation for their failure, He replied, "Because of the littleness of your faith." He then went on to say, "If you have faith as a mustard seed, you shall say to this mountain, 'Move from here to there,' and it shall move; and nothing shall be impossible to you" (Matt. 17:20). Apparently the disciples didn't even have faith the size of a mustard seed! But if all it takes is mustard-seed faith to move a mountain, how much faith would have been enough to cast out a demon? And how much faith would have been enough to heal Bill?

To answer the question, "How much faith is enough?" requires that we do some legwork in our Bibles. Matthew 17:20 provides us with an important piece of the puzzle, but it is only one piece. From that verse it is clear that faith *is* a factor in whether or not our prayers are answered, in whether or not our mountains are moved. Yet we are never given a full-blown doctrine on any subject in just one verse. We always need to consider the whole context of Scripture before concluding what the Bible does or doesn't teach. There isn't space to consider everything the Bible teaches about faith, prayer, and miracles. Instead we will examine a cross section of passages to get an overview of the subject. So get your Bible out, and let's go to work!

The Biblical Data on Faith and Miracles
Matthew 9:27-30 is a passage that seems to corroborate what Jesus said about faith in Matthew 17:20:

And as Jesus passed on from there, two blind men followed Him, crying out, and saying, "Have mercy on us, Son of David!" And after He had come into the house, the blind men came up to Him, and Jesus said to them, "Do you believe that I am able to do this?" They said to Him, "Yes, Lord." Then He touched their eyes, saying, "Be it done to you according to your faith." And their eyes were opened.

From this incident it would seem that there is a direct relationship between the faith and the healing of the ailing individual. The blind men were healed by Jesus because of their faith in Him.

Another story with a similar thrust is the healing of the centurion's slave, in Luke 7:1-10. Jesus was in Capernaum when some Jewish elders sent from a Roman centurion approached Him. One of the centurion's favorite slaves was about to die; and hearing about the power of Jesus, the centurion dispatched these elders to entreat Jesus to heal the slave. The elders deeply respected the Roman centurion, and their emotional pleas persuaded Jesus to go with them.

On the way to the centurion's home, Jesus was again approached, this time by some of the centurion's friends. Their message to Jesus was that He shouldn't trouble Himself to come to the centurion's home. The centurion didn't consider himself worthy to have Jesus under his roof. And from his own experience as a military leader, the centurion reasoned that Jesus would need only to give the word, that He could heal from a distance as easily as from close up.

And when Jesus heard this, He marveled at him, and turned and said to the multitude that was following Him, "I say to you, not even in Israel have I found such great faith." And when those who had been sent returned to the house, they found the slave in good health (vv. 9-10).

Once again faith was instrumental in healing. Also, the centurion was said by Jesus to have not just a little faith but greater than He had found anywhere in Israel.

Yet there is one difference to be noted. In this instance, the person having faith was *not* the person who was healed. Someone else's faith was instrumental in the individual's healing. Apparently the miraculous power of God can work in my life, even if the faith which God responds to is not my own.

The story of the healing of the paralytic in Luke 5:17-26 yields the same conclusion. Again the setting was Capernaum. Jesus was preaching to a large crowd of people inside a house. Outside the house was a man confined by paralysis to a pallet, unable to get in to see or hear Jesus because of the crowd. But this paralytic had a few ingenious friends who weren't about to be stopped by a crowd. They climbed onto the roof of the house—carrying their paralyzed friend with them—removed some of the tiles from the roof, and lowered their friend through the roof right into the middle of the room where Jesus was teaching.

"And seeing their faith, He said 'Friend, your sins are forgiven you' " (v. 20).

Whose faith did Jesus respond to? From the context it is clear that Jesus was referring primarily to the faith of the paralytic's friends, the ones who had so persistently labored to get the paralytic an audience with Jesus. The faith of the paralytic was never mentioned in the passage, not even when Jesus healed his lameness (v. 24).

What an encouragement for those of us who want so desperately for God to work, not just in our own lives but also in the lives of others! By our faith, we can see the power of God released in the life of a brother, a parent, a child, or a business associate. By our faith, the life of another person can be influenced for God.

There are still three more passages that warrant consideration. The first of these is in Luke 7:11-15, which immediately follows the story of the centurion's slave.

> And it came about soon afterwards, that He went to a city called Nain; and His disciples were going along with Him, accompanied by a large multitude.
>
> Now as He approached the gate of the city, behold a dead man was being carried out, the only son of his mother, and she was a widow; and a sizeable crowd from the city was with her.
>
> And when the Lord saw her, He felt compassion for her, and said to her "Do not weep." And He came up and touched the coffin; and the bearers came to a halt. And He said, "Young man, I say to you, arise!" And the dead man sat up, and began to speak. And Jesus gave him back to his mother.

While it is always hazardous to draw a conclusion on the basis of Scripture's silence, I believe we are justified in noticing what is missing in this story—any mention of faith. Obviously, the dead son could not have had faith in Jesus and the mother never got a chance to respond to Jesus in any way. There is no indication that she had ever met Jesus before, or had even heard of Him.

Yet though no one was said to have faith, Jesus raised the boy from the dead. God does not limit Himself by the absence of our faith, when it is His will to act.

One of the most humorous incidents in the Bible is recorded in Acts 12. "So Peter was kept in the prison, but prayer for him was being made fervently by the church to God" (v. 5). The following verses tell us that God, in response to the prayers of the church, miraculously led Peter out of prison at night by means of an angel. Peter couldn't believe the miracle himself at first, but after a few moments he began to realize that he wasn't dreaming.

And when he realized this, he went to the house of Mary, the mother of John who was also called Mark, where many were gathered together and were praying. And when he knocked at the door of the gate, a servant-girl named Rhoda came to answer.

And when she recognized Peter's voice, because of her joy she did not open the gate, but ran in and announced that Peter was standing in front of the gate. And they said to her, "You are out of your mind!" But she kept insisting that it was so. And they kept saying, "It is his angel."

But Peter continued knocking; and when they had opened, they saw him and were amazed (vv. 12-16).

This is hardly the picture of expectant faith! Imagine Rhoda in her excitement slamming the gate on Peter and rushing in to tell the church the good news: "Guess what, everyone—God has answered our prayers! Peter is free!" And how did the church react? Did they say, "Praise God! We knew He would answer our prayers"?

Not at all. Their response was, "Rhoda, you're hallucinating. Peter is in prison. You don't think Herod would have let him out already, do you? Don't be silly!"

From their reaction to Rhoda, I am not overly impressed with the faith of the early church. Yet, even though their faith was less than expectant, God answered their prayers.

But that only brings me back to my initial question: How much faith is enough? Certainly our prayer group had more faith that Bill would be healed than the early church did that Peter would be released from prison, or so it seemed to us. Yet God answered their prayers and said no to ours. Why?

One other passage we dare not ignore is Hebrews 11, the "faith chapter" which records instance after instance of how God responded to the faith of the Old Testament saints by working great miracles. It defines and illustrates the meaning of faith. Yet Hebrews 11 ends in a rather unexpected fashion.

And what more shall I say? For time will fail me if I tell of Gideon, Barak, Samson, Jephthah, of David and Samuel and the prophets, who by faith conquered kingdoms, performed acts of righteousness, obtained promises, shut the mouths of lions, quenched the power of fire, escaped the edge of the sword, from weakness were made strong, became mighty in war, put foreign armies to flight. Women received back their dead by resurrection. . . .

So far, so good. Faith comes out on top. But notice how the author shifts gears with this next statement.

. . . and others were tortured, not accepting their release, in order that they might obtain a better resurrection; and others experienced mockings and scourgings, yes, also chains and imprisonment. They were stoned, they were sawn in two, they were tempted, they were put to death with the sword; they went about in sheepskins, in goatskins, being destitute, afflicted, ill-treated, (men of whom the world was not worthy), wandering in deserts and mountains and caves and holes in the ground.

And all these, having gained approval through their faith, did not receive what was promised, because God had provided something better for us, so that apart from us they should not be made perfect (vv. 32-40).

From verse 35 on the author describes disaster after disaster experienced by people of faith. For no amount of faith was enough to deliver them from pain and death. No amount of faith was enough to enable these heroes of faith to enter what God had promised them. Hebrews 11:13 says, "All these died in faith, without receiving the promises, but having seen them and having welcomed them from a distance." If these heroes of the faith, Abraham, Noah, Sarah, Isaiah, Moses, and Jeremiah, didn't have enough faith to receive God's promises, then who does?

What Have We Learned?

It's time to pull together the biblical data and draw some conclusions about what the Bible really teaches concerning faith, prayer, and miracles.

First, the question, "How much faith is enough?" really misses the point. It intimates that God is something like a celestial vending machine, and that if we just put enough coins of faith in, He will eventually pay off with a miracle. God is not a machine we manipulate by pushing the right buttons. God will not be pressured by our intense faith into performing a miracle.

Rather than reacting to the *pressure* of faith, God in His graciousness responds to the *presence* of faith. What God expects of us when we pray is that faith be present. It doesn't need to be the fully developed faith of a spiritual muscleman who by his years of walking with God has grown to trust in God without reservation in every circumstance. It might be only the frail faith of a spiritual infant who has been so recently reborn that he only understands that Jesus loves him enough to die for him. For God to answer our prayers, faith must be present, even if it's only faith the size of a mustard seed, the smallest seed known in the ancient world.

When the early church prayed for Peter's release, they did not have a complete faith that never doubted for a second that God would answer their prayers. But it was faith, mustard-seed faith, and that's all that God asks.

Second, we must acknowledge that God's power is not limited by our faith. As He did with the deceased son of the widow of Nain, God may choose to act even if there isn't the hint of mountain-moving faith. If God acted only when people exhibited faith in His power, the universe would never have been created and Jesus would still be in the grave.

All of which leads us to the obvious conclusion: faith is not the only factor in whether or not God performs miracles in answer to our prayers. The power of faith to move the mountain is tempered by two other factors —the power of evil in our world and God's own secret purposes.

While Jesus Christ did defeat Satan and death by His resurrection, and while God will ultimately eradicate every vestige of evil from the world, Satan and evil presently continue to have a pervading influence on our lives. Even people who have been miraculously healed by God continue to be plagued by evil. Except for Jesus, every person who was raised from death by God's power eventually died again. And unless Jesus returns first, all of us will die, no matter how much faith we have.

The Book of Revelation describes the ultimate defeat of Satan and evil. It also describes an intense warfare between the forces of evil and the people of God, resulting in suffering and death for many Christians. The truth is that faith cannot always move the mountain, because God in His sovereignty has chosen to allow evil to exert a significant influence in the world.

The reason Satan ever gained a foothold in our world was because of sin—Adam's sin, my sin, and yours. Adam opened the door and we have all had dealings with Satan. God has promised to kick him out again, but not just yet. Until He does, Satan will win some of the battles. Some mountains will remain in our lives.

Other mountains will remain in our lives because God thinks it best that they should. We need to remember that it is God's purpose that we become holy. And this is more important to God than that we be happy. God isn't against happiness, but it's not His top priority for us. Holiness is. And to help us grow in holiness, God often uses a mountain that won't budge, no matter how much faith we have in His power to move it.

We don't always understand God's purposes, but we do know that His purposes are always for our good. In his book, *How Much Faith Does It Take?* Arnold Prater relates the story of a Christian woman named Dana. Dana was great with child, and became even greater when the baby hadn't been delivered three weeks after its due date. The doctor explained to Dana that the baby was healthy but hadn't dropped into position for the journey through the birth canal.

Dana prayed for the baby to drop. In recounting the story, Arnold Prater says that had it been his wife, he would have enlisted as many prayer chains as possible to pray that the baby would drop. The baby stayed right where it was.

> Finally, the doctor decided to deliver by cesarean section and found the baby's umbilical cord twisted around his neck. If he had lowered into position, he would have strangled!
>
> There was no way anyone could have known about that. X rays would not have revealed it. Only God knew. He answered all their prayers with the best possible answer under the circumstances (Thomas Nelson Publishers, pp. 19-20).

How grateful we should be to have a God who is wise enough and good enough not to always answer our prayers exactly as we pray them! How comforting to know that our God will do what is best for us. As the author of Hebrews reminds us, sometimes God doesn't move the mountain because He has something better for us (11:40). We will not always understand what God does, why He allows us to suffer when our faith in Him is so strong. Yet we can be sure that whatever God's reasons, they are designed to give us something better than what we desired.

The Mystery Remains

I would like to be able to understand and explain everything the Bible teaches about the prayer of faith. While I understand something about it, much is still a mystery to me. In his chapter, "Petitionary Prayer: A Problem Without an Answer," C.S. Lewis points out that the Bible teaches two forms of prayer. On the one hand, we are to pray that God's will be done, and then to put our faith in God's wisdom and power to do what is best. And yet we are also taught to pray with an unquestioning faith that God will do the exact thing we ask Him to do. In this regard, Lewis quotes Mark 11:23: "Truly I say to you, whoever says to this mountain, 'Be taken up and cast into the sea,' and does not doubt in his heart, but believes that what he says is going to happen, it shall be granted him." Says Lewis:

> There is no doubt at all that what we are to believe is precisely that we get "all the things" we ask for. We are not to believe that we shall get either what we ask or else something far better: we are to believe that we shall get those very things. It is a faith, unwavering faith in that event, to which success is promised (*Christian Reflections*: Wm. B. Eerdmans, p. 147).

On the other hand, Lewis also acknowledges that just as Jesus prayed in the garden "If it be Thy will," we too should pray in deference to God's greater wisdom and His unquestioned goodness. To assume that in our finiteness and sinfulness we can know better than God what is best is pure foolishness.

Then how should we pray? Should we say, "If it be Thy will"? Or should we pray without doubting for a nanosecond that God will do exactly as we ask? The Bible teaches both patterns, and therein lies the mystery.

Of course, there is more than one mystery in the Bible. Paul calls the incarnation of Jesus a great mystery (1 Tim. 3:16). In heaven we will understand these mysteries. On earth we must learn to live with and appreciate the tension they bring.

Mark Twain once said, "It's not the parts of the Bible I don't understand that trouble me; it's the parts I do understand." While there is much we don't understand about the prayer of faith, there is also much we do understand. We should focus on implementing the answers we do have.

We know that we are to pray with faith. We know that God in His grace often chooses to respond to our faith by performing a miracle. We know that God in His wisdom often chooses not to answer the prayer of faith in exactly the manner we stated our prayer. We know that God hears our prayers, does what is best, and loves us with an immeasurable love. Let's take faith in what we do know. That will be enough!

8 Faith Born From Doubt

Tagging annoyingly behind faith, like an unwanted little brother tracking one's every move, is doubt. No discussion of faith would be complete without giving some consideration to the matter of doubt.

There are two reasons why doubt plays such an important and ubiquitous role in our lives. First, we doubt because our knowledge is limited. We are finite creatures who can never know everything about everything. In the light of our limited knowledge, we will always experience the doubt of uncertainty. For example, because we can never know everything there is to know about the medications we consume, or about the long-term effects of exposure to low-level radiation, we will always have some doubts about their effectiveness and safety.

A second reason for the universality of doubt is the fact that we are a fallen people. The Fall of humanity in the Garden of Eden radically altered the constitution of the universe. We now live in a world of both good and evil. And within each person there is both good and evil. Thus it is only human for us to have doubts about each other. Knowing our own capacity for telling lies, and for failing to fulfill promises made with the best of intentions, we also know that our neighbor is just as capable of deceit and human frailty.

The Bible teaches that sin has affected every part of our lives—our behavior, speech, desires, will, emotions, and our minds. Because sin has significantly affected our minds and emotions, it is impossible for any human being to completely eradicate doubt. Wherever there is faith, Satan is at work planting the seeds of doubt.

Yet doubt does have a sunny side as well. In a world tainted by evil, it is crucial that we not believe everything. Doubt aids us in distinguishing truth from error. Jesus called Satan the "father of lies," and Paul said that Satan is able to disguise himself as an angel of light. Doubt enables us to detect Satan's deceitfulness and to discover God's truth.

In fact, it often happens that the strongest faith is born from doubt. The faith that is able to endure disappointment and hardship has already thoroughly dealt with doubt. The faith that is able to move mountains has learned from experience how to stare down doubt. The strongest faith can be born from the most despairing doubt.

Because doubt is universal, it is vital that we understand something about its nature and how to handle it. Before outlining a plan for dealing with doubt, let's first examine more carefully what doubt is and what causes it.

What Is Doubt?

It is of great importance to recognize that *doubt is not sin*. Doubt is not the opposite of faith. Rather, unbelief is the opposite of faith. Doubt stands between faith and unbelief as fear stands between courage and cowardice.

Think of people who have performed acts of courage. As

I see it, parachuting out of a plane would take a good deal of courage. While I have yet to go parachuting—and I hope my wife will never let me—my friends who have done it tell me that they were as frightened as could be the first few times they jumped. Fear is not incompatible with courage. The courageous person acts, even though he is afraid. He learns to control his fear rather than letting fear control him. The coward is the one whose fear controls him. The opposite of courage is cowardice, not fear.

In much the same way, the opposite of faith is unbelief, not doubt. Faith is an unreserved commitment, a willful choice to obey. Unbelief is a willful refusal to believe or a deliberate decision to disobey. Doubt is torn between wanting to believe and obey and wanting to disbelieve and disobey.

As Os Guinness puts it, to doubt is to be in two minds:

> To believe is to be "in one mind" about accepting something as true; to disbelieve is to be "in one mind" about rejecting it. To doubt is to waver between the two, to believe and disbelieve at once and so to be "in two minds."

Guinness also points out that the core issue regarding doubt is the matter of *trust*.

> Doubt is not primarily an abstract philosophical or theological question, nor a state of morbid spiritual or psychological anguish. At its most basic, doubt is a matter of truth, trust, and trustworthiness. Can we trust God? Are we sure? How can we be sure? (*In Two Minds*, InterVarsity Press, pp. 25, 15)

Without trust, there can be no relationship with God. Yet trust does not spring spontaneously from nothing. There must be some basis for trust, some reasons to trust, some evidence that trust is warranted. And this is precisely where doubt earns its keep. Doubt—which is spelled with a question mark—compels us to ask the questions that are so necessary in order for us to develop a relationship of trust with God. Doubt asks: "Is there a God? What is the evidence for His existence? How do I know what God is like? How can I know that God loves me?"

As those questions are answered, faith comes to life. Trust is born. As doubt seeks and probes and searches for reasons to trust, and as answers are uncovered by doubt's persistence, the foundation for faith is laid. Trust is developed. A relationship begins.

Doubt is a hesitancy to trust until it knows more. As such, it is a valid and beneficial state of mind. It was valid for my wife to want to know more about me before she married me. It was valid for her to hesitate until she had enough information.

Yet, doubt can also become unhealthy and destructive. There comes a point when our doubts have been provided sufficient data and a decision is in order. Doubt which is destructive continues to hesitate, refuses to decide, and persists in remaining "in two minds" when the time to choose has come and gone.

While doubt does have its sunny side, we are all too aware that doubt is an unhappy state. It is not pleasant to be caught in a question mark, to be strung out on the highwire between faith and unbelief. Because doubt is often painful, it urges us toward a resolution. It demands that we take action to remedy the uncertainty and the accompanying frustration. Doubt demands action.

The Derivations of Doubt
The first step in dealing with a doubt is to identify its source. Not all doubts spring from the same well. Sometimes we

doubt because we lack information. Sometimes we doubt because our emotions have come unglued. Sometimes we doubt because the information we have gathered is flawed by error. Let me suggest derivations of doubt.

• I have already mentioned the doubt that comes from honest questioning, that can't decide because it doesn't know enough of the facts. These doubts can be beneficial to us by motivating us to actively pursue information that will resolve our doubts and build up our faith.

• A second type is the doubt we experience when God doesn't do what we expect Him to. This was the source of John the Baptist's doubts about Jesus. "Now when John in prison heard of the works of Christ, he sent word by his disciples, and said to Him, "Are You the Coming One, or shall we look for someone else?" (Matt. 11:2-3)

At first reading, that question seems to be a rather odd one for John the Baptist to ask. After all, John was the forerunner of Jesus, the one who had been sent specially by God to prepare Israel for the coming of the Messiah. Even while John was in his mother's womb, he seemed to know that Jesus was the Messiah.

> When Elizabeth heard Mary's greeting, the baby moved within her. Elizabeth was filled with the Holy Spirit and said in a loud voice, "You are the most blessed of all women, and blessed is the Child you will bear! Why should this great thing happen to me, that my Lord's mother comes to visit me? For as soon as I heard your greeting, the baby within me jumped with gladness" (Luke 1:41-44, GNB).

If John had any doubts about who the Messiah was when he was beginning his ministry, they disappeared when John saw Jesus in the Jordan River.

The next day John saw Jesus coming to him, and said: "There is the Lamb of God, who takes away the sin of the world! This is the One I was talking about when I said, 'A Man is coming after me, but He is greater than I am, because He existed before I was born.' I did not know who He would be but I came baptizing with water in order to make Him known to the people of Israel."

And John gave this testimony: "I saw the Spirit come down like a dove from heaven and stay on Him. I still did not know that He was the One, but God, who sent me to baptize with water, had said to me, 'You will see the Spirit come down and stay on a Man; He is the one who baptizes with the Holy Spirit.' I have seen it," said John, "and I tell you that He is the Son of God" (John 1:29-34, GNB).

How can it be that the same John who was so certain that Jesus was the Christ, the Messiah, the Son of God, could doubt Him enough to dispatch his followers to pointedly ask Jesus who He was? For John, being in prison wasn't the worst of his plight. The worst of it was his doubt about whether the one he had staked his life on was really who He claimed to be.

John's doubts were those which develop when God doesn't do what we expect Him to. The Jewish people were expecting a very different Messiah than the one they got in Jesus of Nazareth. They anticipated that the Messiah would restore Israel to power, unseat the Roman rulers, destroy the wicked, avenge the righteous, and usher in the kingdom of God with peace, power, and prosperity.

But so far, little had changed. Jesus had performed some miracles, but so had Elijah and Elisha. The Romans were still in power, the nation of Israel was still oppressed; and worst of all, the one who had been sent by God to pave the way for the coming of the triumphant Messiah had been tossed into prison! As John slumped on the cold prison floor, the faith and confidence that had once burned so brightly now lay in ashes: "Are You the Coming One, or shall we look for someone else?"

When God doesn't do what we expect Him to do, the doubt that has been silently tagging along behind us quickly makes its voice heard. When the mountain we expected God to move remains as an imposing obstacle to our hopes and dreams, doubt speaks up. When we implore God to send us an answer and hear only silence echoing through the night, doubt whispers, "Can you trust God? Are you sure? How can you be sure? Why should you trust God when He doesn't seem to listen to you?"

• A third variety is the doubt of forgetfulness. Os Guinness labels this the doubt of ingratitude. It defiantly declares, "Why do I need God? What has He done for me? Why should I obey God when I can handle life just fine by myself?"

Moses warned the people of Israel about succumbing to this type of doubt:

> Beware lest you forget the Lord your God by not keeping His commandments and His ordinances and His statutes which I am commanding you today; lest, when you have eaten and are satisfied, and have built good houses and lived in them, and when your herds and your flocks multiply, and your silver and gold multiply, and all that you have multiplies, then your heart becomes proud, and you forget the Lord your God who brought you out from the land of Egypt, out of the house of slavery.... Otherwise, you may say in your heart, "My power and the strength of my hand made me this wealth" (Deut. 8:11-14, 17).

It isn't just the non-Christian who doesn't see any need for God. Even as Christians we occasionally fall into the same blind way of thinking. We forget what God has done for us and given us. When God's work in our lives fades into the shadows, the doubts we have of His presence and power waft to the fore.

• A fourth type of doubt is derived from inherited beliefs. This is the peculiar doubt of the person who has grown up in a Christian home, been educated in a Christian school system, and who has been a faithful and active church member from the nursery on up. Suddenly this person is confronted with a question about God or the Bible by a professor or a friend who doesn't share his faith, a question that the long-time Christian can't immediately answer. Before long the unanswered question spawns a whole host of doubts about the reliability of the Bible and the existence of God; and the person's faith may collapse like a row of dominoes.

The reason these doubts develop in the first place is that so many professing Christians have never really decided for themselves whether to believe in God and to trust Jesus Christ as their Saviour. They inherited their beliefs and values from parents or friends, without ever examining the evidence supporting those beliefs. They believed what they were taught about God, because there never seemed to be any reason not to believe.

But when someone came along who was able to give what seemed a solid reason not to believe, their faith came tumbling down. They hadn't built their faith step by step, but had bought the whole package at once, no questions asked.

The problem with inherited beliefs is that there are no answers to give, because no questions have been asked. The person whose faith is nothing more than inherited beliefs is dangerously susceptible to crippling doubts.

• A fifth family of doubt is the type most troublesome to me. It is the doubt from lack of growth. Every now and then I experience a time in my spiritual life when my relationship with God is as dry as a dead leaf, as energizing as a tranquilizer. Either I pray and see nothing happen, or I don't feel like praying, so I don't. I know that I should be growing, that I should be loving God more, that I should be serving Him more effectively, yet absolutely nothing seems to be happening. So I ask myself, "What's going on? Where's the power and the thrill? Why isn't anything changing? Where did God go?"

• The sixth type of doubt comes from unruly emotions. It's the doubt we experience because we're physically exhausted and emotionally spent. First Kings 19 chronicles the story of the Prophet Elijah, who was so depressed and so shrouded in doubt that he wanted only to die. Much of the reason for his psychological and spiritual condition was weariness. He was physically fatigued and emotionally wrung out. Doubts catch up with us quickly when our emotions go haywire and sap our strength to resist. When unpleasant circumstances converge with those erupting emotions, our faith is sometimes kidnapped and thrown out of office.

Dealing With Doubt

There are other families of doubt than the six already discussed. In dealing with a doubt, our first step is to identify its origin. Just as doctors prescribe different medications to combat various viruses, so different types of doubt must be treated according to their causes.

The second step in dealing with a doubt is to express it, to get it out into the open. For some reason many Christians have developed the notion that doubt is something to be covered up like age-spots or facial blemishes. Yet that is the *worst* thing we can do with our doubts.

Did you ever have one of those old black and white television sets, the kind that had a wire hanger for an antenna and required the use of a fork or a screwdriver to change the channels? We once had an old set on which we could never get a clear picture. Either there were shadows or the picture was fuzzy or the horizontal control would go on the blink. Just when we would think we had it adjusted right and would start to enjoy a big game, the picture would go spastic.

A person with a set like that had three options. He could watch the fuzzy picture and listen to the sound, imagining what the real picture might look like. That got frustrating very quickly. Or he could spend the money to have the set fixed so that it would work right. Or he could turn off the set, roll it into the closet, and forget about it.

When we have doubts, our picture of God has gone out of focus. It has gotten fuzzy and blurred so that we don't see Him clearly. When this happens, we have options similar to the person with the faulty TV set. We can leave the picture fuzzy, or we can fix what is wrong. Or, if we think that to doubt is to sin, we can simply pack up our doubts, roll them into the closet, and try to pretend that they don't exist. Yet when we do that, our image of God never gets cleared up. The picture will always be distorted and we will never see Him as He really is.

Doubts can be a springboard to faith, but only if we face them squarely and openly. If you have doubts, don't try to hide them. Get them out in the open instead of hiding them in the closet. Tell someone you trust about your doubts. You'll probably discover that your friend has had doubts at some time.

After identifying your doubt and expressing it openly, the third step is to take action to resolve it. Pascal once said:

> Doubt then is an unhappy state,
> but there is an indispensable duty to seek in doubt,
> and thus anyone who doubts and does not seek

is at once unhappy and in the wrong
(Os Guinness, *In Two Minds*, p. 49).

What action can a doubting person take? That depends on the specific brand of doubt. The person who doubts because of honest questions needs to read some books dealing with his questions, to ask other Christians how they resolved their doubts—in other words, to do some research. After 2,000 years, all the basic questions about Christianity have been asked and have been answered, to some degree or another. No one is going to come up with a new question that will send the Christian faith tumbling. There are answers that are thorough and reasonable, even if not always exhaustive, to every question the skeptic and the doubter might have.

The person whose doubts spring from unruly emotions needs patience, a good meal, some time to relax, and a few good nights of sleep. The person whose doubts derive from forgetfulness should spend some time recalling what God has done, both for him and for God's people in history.

If you have doubts, perhaps the most helpful action you can take is to find a trustworthy, mature Christian friend with whom you can talk honestly and even debate. Talk out your doubts, your frustrations, your anger, your hurt, your questions. Often just talking will cure what ails you, and your friend may be able to share some ideas that have helped him navigate his way through the turmoil of doubt.

The fourth step to take in dealing with doubt is to simply *decide*. There comes a point when the answers and the information are sufficient to enable you to choose whether you will believe or not believe. Faith is an active decision. You don't fall into faith. You choose faith. Ultimately, doubt is resolved only by a conscious decision: Will you believe?

Faith Born From Doubt

Perhaps the most famous of all doubters is the Apostle Thomas, better known as Doubting Thomas. When Jesus appeared to the disciples after His resurrection, Thomas was not with them. When they told him the fantastic news that Jesus was alive, Thomas replied, "Unless I shall see in His hands the imprint of the nails, and put my finger into the place of the nails, and put my hand into His side, I will not believe" (John 20:25).

Thomas had some hard-core doubts. It was difficult for his analytical mind to accept that a person he had seen crucified and buried only a few days earlier was alive.

Eight days later Jesus appeared again, and this time Thomas was there. Jesus didn't condemn Thomas for his doubts. He didn't chastise him and tell him that because of his doubts he could never again be a disciple. He simply said, "Reach here your finger, and see My hands; and reach here your hand, and place it into My side; and be not unbelieving, but believing." And what did Thomas say? "My Lord and my God!" (vv. 27-28)

When Thomas came face to face with the evidence—and with Jesus—he became a believer. Tradition tells us that Thomas carried the message of the resurrected Jesus all the way to southern India, farther than any other disciple. The faith born from doubt proved to be a faith of strength, dedication, daring, and endurance.

Our God is willing to receive us with our doubts, to give us grace to be honest with them and to honestly seek Him. And He can use those doubts to make us even stronger in our faith. The strongest faith is often born out of the most despairing doubt. When in doubt—take faith!

9 Faith, Decision-Making, and Morality

Making decisions is a part of daily life. Many of the decisions we make each day are *nonmoral*; that is, they don't involve choosing between right and wrong. Deciding what clothes to wear, what cereal to eat for breakfast, when to have lunch, how to spend our leisure time, and what TV program to watch before bedtime—these are nonmoral decisions.

There are a few major decisions we make in our lives that are much more important than deciding what to wear, but which still remain outside the scope of morality. Deciding if, who, and when to marry is a critically important decision requiring a great deal of deliberation. Yet it is not a choice between right and wrong, between holiness and sinfulness. Deciding on a school to attend, a major to study, a career to pursue, a house to purchase—these are examples of profound and complex decisions that are nonmoral in nature.

There are choices we are called to make which are *moral* in nature, involving right and wrong. Often these decisions are loaded with emotion and are as perplexing to the biblical scholar as to the lay person. Often these decisions, because of their complexity and because of what is at stake, tend to promote devisiveness and dissension. Examples of very difficult moral decisions are:

• Should I have an abortion?

• Should I divorce my alcoholic, unfaithful husband?

• Should our church protest the nuclear arms race, or should we encourage our leaders to build an even stronger defense?

• Should I go to war, when called on by my government, no matter what the circumstances of the conflict?

• Should our church lead or impede the effort of American women to legislate equal rights and equal pay for women?

• Should we make every effort medically possible to maintain my aged mother's life, or should we allow her to die naturally and peacefully?

Not all moral choices are as emotionally charged or as hazardous as these examples. More common choices are:

• Is it right for me to attend that movie?

• Is it right to allow my children to watch those TV programs?

• Is this an ethical method to use in closing a business deal?

• How physically involved should we be before marriage?

• Is it acceptable to have wine with dinner, or is it always wrong to drink alcohol?

• Is it moral to spend my money on luxuries when 16,000 people die every day from hunger and hunger-related diseases?

All moral decisions, whether they are matters of life and death or not, are difficult. All of them are important to the person serious about his commitment to Jesus Christ. All of them require diligent study and careful thought.

The bottom-line decision is whether I will obey God or choose my own way. If I decide that the way I use my money is immoral, or that the way I conduct my business is unethical, the critical decision remains: Will I change? Will I be obedient to what I believe is right and just, or will I go on living as I have? This type of decision is one that I make daily. And if I am honest I must admit that I don't always decide to do what I know and believe is right.

Every moral decision is difficult. To make wise decisions and correct moral choices demands patience, persistence, courage, determination, logic, honesty, and prudence. It also demands faith.

The need for faith in making correct moral choices might not at first seem apparent. The need for logic seems reasonable. Prudence and courage seem to fit. But what does faith have to do with choosing a marriage partner? What does faith have to do with the issue of divorce? What does faith have to do with whether or not I give money to the church?

To discover the role of faith in decision-making and morality, we'll look first at the role faith plays in our nonmoral decisions, and then examine the relationship between faith and morality.

Faith and Decision-Making

• In making nonmoral decisions, we can first take faith that God has given us freedom to choose. Unless God supernaturally reveals to us that we are to decide one way or the other, we are completely free to choose, not only what to wear and eat but also whom to marry and what career to pursue. As long as our choices are made with the motive of glorifying God and making use of our spiritual gifts, and as long as we do not violate God's moral will in what we choose, we are free to choose according to our own preferences and judgment.

Decision-making, especially when it involves matters such as marriage and vocation, is often an exasperating process. As Christians we have tended in the past to intensify the agony of making decisions by believing that it was imperative to discover God's perfect plan for us as individuals, and that if we missed God's perfect plan by marrying the "wrong" person we would be guilty of sin as well as of having made an error in judgment.

Believing that there is one "right" career for me to pursue, that God knows what that "right" career is, and that my task is to figure out what it is, turns what is really a nonmoral decision into a moral one. So if I decide to marry Jean instead of Laura—when Laura was really God's perfect choice for me—then by marrying Jean I have sinned against God and blown my chance of knowing God's best for my life!

While I was always uncomfortable with that particular concept of God's will, it was what I had been taught. I believed that it was necessary for me to somehow find out whether or not it was God's will for me to move to San Diego or to Chicago. I believed that it was crucial to discover if it was God's will for me to get married. And it was critical to discern whether God wanted me to be a pastor.

I had two problems, though, with the belief that God had a perfect plan for every detail of my life and that it was my task to find out what that plan was, piece by piece, as I proceeded through life. For one, I could never figure out *how* God was supposed to tell me His will. I never did feel led or called or moved by the Spirit to go to San Diego. I finally decided to make the move because it seemed to be the best way for me to grow in my faith, minister to hurting people, and get more sun that I could in Minnesota. In retrospect, I believe it was a very wise decision. But I could never honestly claim that I made that decision because it was God's will for me.

Besides the practical problem of not knowing just how God was going to reveal His detailed will for my life, I could never find in Scripture that God does have a detailed, explicit plan for my life. While I believe in God's sovereignty and in the doctrine of predestination, I don't believe God promises to explain to me who I should marry, where I should live, or what I should do for a career. Rather, the Bible tells me that God has given me freedom to choose in the nonmoral areas of my life according to my own preferences and judgment. (For a fuller discussion of this concept, see *Decision-Making and the Will of God*, Multnomah Press, 1980).

Right from the Garden of Eden, God gave His people freedom to choose: "And the Lord commanded the man, saying, 'From any tree of the garden you may eat freely; but from the tree of the knowledge of good and evil you shall not eat, for in the day that you eat from it you shall surely die'" (Gen. 2:16-17).

To Adam and Eve God gave the freedom to choose from any tree in the garden except one. There are certain actions we are not free to choose. Those are the actions God specifically forbids. But if God has not forbidden it, and if the principles of the Bible do not lead us to believe that a certain concern is a matter of right and wrong, then God seems to tell us, "Choose what you want! Do what you think best! When you are pleased, I am pleased!"

To have faith that God has given us freedom to choose according to our own preferences and judgment relieves us of the anxiety caused by the fruitless effort to unearth God's perfect plan. Making wise decisions is a difficult enough task without the added burden of worrying whether or not we are sinning against God, in areas where He has not expressed His will.

• In making nonmoral decisions, we can take faith that

God has already revealed all we need to know about His will. First Thessalonians 4:3 plainly states, "For this is the will of God, your sanctification; that is, that you abstain from sexual immorality." In the context it is clear that God's will for us is that we be holy, that we set ourselves apart from sin.

Paul indicated why he prayed that the church would know God's will:

> For this reason also, since the day we heard of it, we have not ceased to pray for you and to ask that you may be filled with the knowledge of His will in all spiritual wisdom and understanding, so that you may walk in a manner worthy of the Lord, to please Him in all respects, bearing fruit in every good work and increasing in the knowledge of God (Col. 1:9-10).

Paul wasn't praying that the Colossians would know God's will so that they could choose the right vocation. He wanted them to know God's will so that they could become more godly, more fruitful in their ministry and so that they would know God more intimately.

If you have been frustrated in trying to find God's will for your life, take faith! Everything you need to know about discovering God's will is already in the Bible. God's will for you is that you live a godly, fruitful life.

• In making nonmoral decisions we can take faith in the fatherhood of God. In Colossians 1:2 Paul said, "Grace to you and peace from God our Father." Jesus taught us to pray, "Our Father" (Matt. 6:9). In Galatians 4:6 we are told, "Because you are sons, God has sent forth the Spirit of His Son into our hearts, crying, 'Abba! Father!' "

How does faith in God's fatherhood affect nonmoral decisions? Gary Friesen explains it this way:

Does the wise father guide his child by formulating a plan that covers every detail of the child's life and then revealing that plan step by step as each decision must be made? Of course not. The father who is truly wise teaches his child the basic principles of life; he teaches what is right and wrong, what is wise against what is foolish. He then seeks to train the child to make his own decisions making proper use of those correct guidelines. Such a father is overjoyed when he knows that the child has matured to the point where he is able to function independently as an adult, making wise decisions on the basis of principles learned in his youth (*Decision-Making and the Will of God*, p. 85).

Because God is our Father, we can be sure that He is going to make known to us everything we need to make our own wise decisions. He won't try to trick or confuse us. Nor will He dictate each move we make or each breath we breathe. As our loving wise Father, He will provide us with the insight and the sensibility to choose wisely. As our Father, God treats us as responsible sons and daughters who can be trusted with the freedom He gives us to choose according to our own desires and judgment. Take faith in the fatherhood of God.

• In making nonmoral decisions we can take faith in God's willingness to give us wisdom. James 1:5 assures us, "But if any of you lacks wisdom, let him ask of God, who gives to all men generously and without reproach, and it will be given to him."

Undoubtedly, wisdom is the quality most needed in making good decisions. The Bible is the most comprehensive source of wisdom we have. The wisest person is the one who best knows, believes, and obeys the truth of Scripture. To get wisdom, to develop the quality of making efficient, sound, profitable decisions, the first step is to study and obey the teachings of the Bible.

Yet God also grants wisdom in answer to prayer. When Solomon asked God to give him the wisdom necessary to rule the people of Israel, God answered his prayer by making him the wisest person in the world (1 Kings 3:9 ff). When you are faced with a decision that seems impossible to make, don't panic. Don't worry. Don't get angry. Believe that in answer to your prayer God will give you the wisdom you need to ferret out the facts, comprehend what is confusing you, and choose confidently.

• In making nonmoral decisions, we can take faith that God can redeem our mistakes. We all make mistakes. We all make foolish decisions. Murphy's Law—"If anything can go wrong, it will"—plagues the president and the post office, as well as the rest of us.

Yet we don't need to let our mistakes incapacitate us or cause us interminable distress. God can redeem our mistakes! The promise of Romans 8:28—"And we know that God causes all things to work together for good to those who love God"—applies to our mistakes as much as to the tragedies of life over which we have no control.

There is no question that mistakes do wear away at us. And some of them are so major that they erode what we are and have. Some Christians have made major mistakes in choosing a marriage partner, and have suffered terribly because of it. Some have made mistakes in business and have lost everything. Yet God can redeem our mistakes.

One of the most majestic, commanding sights in all the world is the Grand Canyon. Its size and beauty are breathtaking. Yet this masterpiece is the product of erosion. Day after day, month after month, year after year, the incessant current of the Colorado River and the careless blowing of the wind have transformed a great plain into a grand canyon. God has used the process of erosion to present us with a spectacular gift.

God can redeem your mistakes. He can use what wears away at you to transform you into someone even more attractive, more capable, more like Jesus. When you make a mistake, don't look at what you've lost. Look at what's left! Take faith in God's ability to redeem your mistakes.

Faith and Morality

Faith relates to the task of making moral decisions in at least three ways.

• In making moral decisions we can take faith that God knows better than we do what is right and what is wrong.

Ethicists distinguish between two basic approaches to moral decisions, the *deontological* and the *teleological*. The names aren't particularly important, but the principles behind them are.

The deontological approach tells us that we must make moral decisions on the basis of the rules. Since God's rule is that we ought not to kill, we ought not to kill. The teleologist encourages us to consider the result of our action in making a moral choice. While the rule says not to kill, if the result of killing is good (for example, if killing a Hitler would save other innocent lives), then to kill in that instance is right.

The teleologist contends that the result determines what the rule is. The deontologist argues that the rule is good regardless of the result.

One of the most well-known examples used by teleologists to support their perspective is Mrs. Bergmeier. During World War II Mrs. Bergmeier, a German, was captured by the Russians. Her husband and two small children survived the Russian attack and fled to safety. While in prison camp, Mrs. Bergmeier was informed that the only way she could be released was to become pregnant. When a Russian guard offered his services, Mrs. Bergmeier was confronted with an unpleasant decision: Should she be faithful to her husband, even if it meant dying, or should she allow the soldier to impregnate her so she could be sent back to her family?

The teleologist says, "Forget the rule about adultery. Look at the results of her action first. If she doesn't become pregnant, she'll probably die and her husband and children will be left alone. If she does, she'll be returned to her family, and give birth to a new life.

The example is a famous one because Mrs. Bergmeier did become pregnant, was reunited with her family, and gave birth to a son who was very special to them.

But while the teleologist bases his moral choices on the results, the deontologist makes his moral choices on the foundation of faith. The fact of the matter is that we don't know all the results of our actions. Only God is able to know the end of the situation as well as the beginning. Only God can see the whole parade at the same time. Only God knew what the consequences of Mrs. Bergmeier's decision would be for her husband, her children, the infant, the Russian soldier, as well as for herself. God is the only Being in the universe capable of being a teleologist. Everyone else is limited by the parameters of finite humanity. It is impossible for us to make a moral choice on the basis of what the results will be, because we can't know what they will be.

By faith the Christian obeys God's rules because he believes that God knows better than he does what is right and what is wrong. As our Creator, God knows how our actions will affect us. He alone knows exactly what is best for us. He has revealed His rules to us, and He asks us to obey them by faith—faith in His wisdom and goodness.

I always have a difficult time trying to convince adolescents that premarital sex is both wrong and unhealthy for them. If I try to dissuade them on the basis of what the results of their actions will be, they usually win the debate. I explain to them the medical risks, the adverse effect it can have on their relationships, the damage it can do to their future, the hurt and the pain it can cause their parents as well as themselves, and on and on. But inevitably someone will object on the grounds that no ill will come of it if they use the proper methods of deterring pregnancy and if they are involved only with a person they love. It's pleasurable, it's an expression of love, and no one is hurt by it, they say.

But God knows better than we do what the results will be. Knowing what He knows, God has instructed us that sex is to be reserved for marriage, that it is an expression of total commitment between two people who are married to each other. According to God, sex in any other context, whether premarital, homosexual, or extramarital, is wrong. God knows that sex outside of marriage is ultimately destructive, and so He has told us to stay away from it.

Because God knows better than we do what's right and what's wrong, we need to take His rules seriously.

• In making moral decisions we can take faith that God will guide us. In His Word, God has promised to help us in choosing between right and wrong, and then in doing right.

Galatians 5:18 says, "But if you are led by the Spirit, you are not under the Law." In Romans 8:14 we read, "For all who are being led by the Spirit of God, these are sons of God." Those verses are often construed as promises that God will lead us in making nonmoral choices. Yet a quick reading of the contexts of those two verses shows that the subject under discussion in each is the battle between a godly and an ungodly life. In Galatians we are promised that if we are led by God's Spirit, we will have love, joy, peace, patience, kindness, goodness, faithfulness, gentleness, and self-control. If we ignore God's leading, the results will be immorality, jealousy, fighting, and impurity.

God's goal for us is that we become godly people. As we confront difficult moral choices, we can be confident that

God will not leave us to our own resources. He won't abandon us as we sincerely struggle to discern right from wrong. By His Holy Spirit living in us, God will lead us into righteousness.

• In making moral choices, we can take faith that God will bless our obedience. Remember, faith is more than just believing the truth. It is also acting on the truth. The person of faith actively obeys what he believes is right, even if doing so yields painful results. He obeys because of his faith that God will somehow use his obedience fruitfully.

Though Rome in the fourth century was officially Christian, the gladiatorial games in which refugees of defeated nations killed each other off, continued. A monk named Telemachus, who had spent most of his life praying and fasting in the desert, arrived in Rome just after General Stilicho had won a great battle over the Goths. Stilicho's prisoners were sent into the arena to entertain 80,000 people by fighting and dying.

Telemachus could not believe what he was seeing. He jumped over the wall and made his way between two gladiators. At the insistence of the supposedly Christian crowd, the gladiators shoved Telemachus out of the way and kept on fighting.

Telemachus knew he could not watch passively as this went on. Again he came between the gladiators. The crowd threw stones at him, the commander of the games gave an order, a sword flashed through the air—and Telemachus was killed.

When the crowd saw what had happened, they fell silent. The games were called to a halt for the day, and were never resumed again. By his act of courage and obedience, Telemachus had put an end to the killing. As one historian commented, "His death was more useful to mankind than his life."

You may never win a medal for standing up for what you believe is right. Your efforts to combat injustice may never achieve what you set out to accomplish. Your obedience to God in the small things of life may never be applauded or even noticed. But God will bless your obedience.

We have seen that faith plays an important role in making decisions. Faith is not an idle spectator passively watching as we struggle to choose. Faith enables us to choose wisely and confidently. And it gives us the courage to do what is right, even when the right thing is very hard.

10 Growing Your Faith—I

How do you go about getting more faith? Is it even possible to grow your faith? Isn't faith a gift from God rather than a product of your own efforts? Something you either have or don't have?

A long time ago I learned that the answers to many of life's most mysterious questions are just as often both/and as they are either/or. The Bible teaches the fact of predestination as well as the fact of a person's freedom to choose and act according to his own individual will. At first glance, the two don't seem to go together. Either God predestines what I will do and I have no choice in the matter, or I am free to do as I choose apart from God's interference. Yet as mutually exclusive as the two concepts may seem, both predestination and free will are taught by Scripture.

Similarly, the Bible teaches that faith is both a gift of God and a capacity that we are responsible to grow and develop. That faith is a gift from God is not open to dispute. Everything we are and have is a gift from God. Our bodies, our abilities, our talents, our opportunities, our material possessions, our families, our jobs—everything is a gift from God, the Creator, the Initiator. Apart from God's initiating activity, faith would be impossible.

Yet Scripture also affirms the truth that we can grow our faith. To the Thessalonians Paul wrote, "We are bound to give thanks to God always for you, brethren, as is fitting, because your faith is growing abundantly" (2 Thes. 1:3, RSV). In 2 Corinthians 10:14-15 Paul alluded to the same truth:

> For we are not overextending ourselves, as if we did not reach to you, for we were the first to come even as far as you in the Gospel of Christ; not boasting beyond our measure, that is, in other men's labors, but with the hope that as your faith grows, we shall be, within our sphere, enlarged even more by you.

Faith is a seed planted in our hearts by God. Like all seeds, it needs to be properly nourished in order to grow. Our task is to care for and nourish the seed of faith so that it can develop into a healthy and dynamic faith capable of moving mountains.

We might also think of faith as a muscle or a habit or an ability. To strengthen our muscles and to develop our abilities requires a good deal of effort on our part. Growth demands exercise, stretching, and practice.

In commenting on the Parable of the Talents, William Barclay challenges us to continued growth. Matthew 25:29 reads, "For to everyone who has shall more be given, and he shall have an abundance; but from the one who does not have, even what he does have shall be taken away." In his explanation of this verse Barclay says:

> It tells us that to him who has more will be given, and he who has not will lose what he has. The meaning is this. If a man

has a talent and exercises it, he is progressively able to do more with it. But, if he has a talent and fails to exercise it, he will inevitably lose it. If we have some proficiency at a game or an art, if we have some gift for doing something, the more we exercise that proficiency and that gift, the harder the work and the bigger the task we will be able to tackle. Whereas, if we fail to use it, we lose it. That is equally true of playing golf or playing the piano, of singing songs or writing sermons, or carving wood or thinking out ideas. It is the lesson of life that the only way to keep a gift is to use it in the service of God and in the service of our fellowmen (*The Gospel of Matthew*, Vol. 2, Westminster Press, p. 324).

Faith is a gift graciously given to us by God. Yet it is our responsibility to use our faith, to exercise it, to stretch it, to develop it. Faith grows as we use it, and the more we use it, the more faith God gives to us.

But how do we use our faith? How do we exercise and stretch it? What can we do to nourish and to cultivate faith?

This chapter and the next propose some specific answers to those questions. The following steps are actions that have proved workable and beneficial to many people who have set out to grow their faith. There is nothing magic about the process. It takes hard and consistent effort, determination, desire, and discipline. But the results are worth the cost!

In this chapter I will concentrate on three of the most essential steps in growing your faith. Seven other suggestions will be given in chapter 11. Knowing what these steps are won't help you a bit; but doing them will change your life.

Step One—Bible Study

The first step in growing your faith is to make a habit of reading and studying the Bible daily. Since faith involves believing the truth about God, it is essential to have a knowledge of God's revelation of truth. Paul said, "So faith comes from hearing, and hearing by the word of Christ" (Rom. 10:17). The seed of faith that God has deposited in our hearts is activated and cultivated as we nourish it with the truth of Scripture. As we study the Bible we will understand more and more about who God is, how He has worked in the lives of people in the past, what He promises to do for us, and how He wants us to live. This understanding provides the content of our faith, without which faith degenerates into positive thinking and emotionalism.

Understanding what the Bible teaches, as vital as that is, is only a part of the process of Bible study. All good Bible study involves three components: analysis, interpretation, and application.

• Analysis answers the question, "What did this passage mean to the original readers?" It is important to remember that the Bible was not written to us. It was written for us, but it was written to specific people in history whose culture and circumstances differed radically from our own. First, then, we must make an effort to understand how the original readers of Genesis, Acts, Romans, Revelation, and each of the other books of the Bible would have understood the messages of those books.

• Interpretation answers the question, "What is the main point of this passage for people of all times? What is the enduring, timeless principle?" For example, in 1 Corinthians 11:1-16, Paul discusses the issue of why women should have their heads covered while praying. The analysis of that passage would show how Christians living in first-century Corinth would have understood Paul's point. The interpretation would distill whatever enduring principle applies to people of all ages and all cultures. One such principle would be that it is vital that our worship services be conducted with order and dignity. That women should cover their heads when they pray in church is most likely not an enduring principle to be drawn from those verses.

• Application answers the question, "What difference will this passage make in my own life? How should I think or act differently because of my understanding of this passage?"

One of my favorite Bible studies to teach is called, "When the Bible Is a Waste of Time." Most of us can think of plenty of things that are a waste of time, but few if any classify reading or studying the Bible in that category. Yet the Parable of the Sower informs us that unless we apply the truth we've learned, unless we respond to the message of the Bible by obeying it, we have really wasted our time in studying it. Look at Jesus' words in the parable:

> The sower went out to sow his seed; and as he sowed, some fell beside the road; and it was trampled under foot, and the birds of the air devoured it. And other seed fell on rocky soil, and as soon as it grew up, it withered away, because it had no moisture. And other seed fell among the thorns; and the thorns grew up with it, and choked it out. And other seed fell into the good ground, and grew up, and produced a crop a hundred times as great (Luke 8:5-8).

Then Jesus explained the parable to His disciples:

> Now the parable is this: the seed is the Word of God. And those beside the road are those who have heard; then the devil comes and takes away the Word from their heart, so that they may not believe and be saved. And those on the rocky soil are those who, when they hear, receive the Word with joy; and these have no firm root; they believe for a while, and in time of temptation fall away. And the seed which fell among thorns, these are the ones who have heard,

and as they go on their way they are choked with worries and riches and pleasures of this life, and bring no fruit to maturity.

And the seed in the good ground, these are the ones who have heard the Word in an honest and good heart, and hold it fast, and bear fruit with perseverance (Luke 8:11-15).

The result God desires in our lives, when we read or hear the Word, is that we bear fruit. The general meaning of that phrase is that we should have changed lives. The change might be in our own lives, as we bear the fruit of the Spirit (Gal. 5:22-23) and become more like Jesus Christ in character. Or the change might be in other people's lives, the fruit of our ministry. The goal of the proclamation of God's Word is that people be brought into a personal relationship with God and then into conformity to the character of Jesus Christ.

The Parable of the Sower teaches that most of the time the Word of God does not accomplish in our lives what it is intended to do. I. Howard Marshall summarizes the Parable by saying, "Hearing the Word must lead to the production of fruit, or else the hearing is in vain." Understanding the message of the Bible without acting on it accomplishes nothing. The only right response to hearing God's Word is to bear fruit, to change, to grow. We might bear fruit by becoming more patient, generous, or kind. We might bear fruit by taking action to heal our neighbor's hurt or share the Gospel message with an unbelieving friend. We might bear fruit by worshiping God more enthusiastically, praying more consistently, or being more grateful to God for His action in our lives.

Karl Marx once said, "The philosophers have only interpreted the world in various ways; the point is to change it." Revising Marx's statement, we might say, "Bible students have often only *interpreted* the Bible in various ways; the point is to be *changed* by it." The people in the Parable of the Sower who failed to produce fruit lacked follow-through. They may have understood the message of God's Word, but for one reason or another their understanding was never translated into action.

Reading and studying the Bible daily is an essential ingredient in nourishing and growing our faith. Yet it is crucial to remember that faith-building Bible study does not end when we have come to understand what the Bible teaches. Understanding is but the beginning. Unless we allow the truth of the Bible to change us, we have wasted our time and disregarded the power of the Word of God. To grow our faith we must take pains to specifically apply the message of Scripture as well as to interpret and understand it.

Step Two—Prayer

As we saw in chapter 2, a major component of faith is trust. We learn to trust people as we take time to be with them and get to know them better. Yet there are two kinds of people we don't trust: people who have demonstrated that they aren't trustworthy, and people we don't know. The Bible assures us that God is trustworthy. Therefore, what limits our trust in God is our personal knowledge of Him. The better and more intimately we know God, the stronger our trust and faith in Him will be.

We know God through the Bible. The Bible helps us to understand what God is like since it is His written revelation. Yet God has also made it possible for us to know and experience Him through prayer. The more time we spend in prayer, the better our relationship with God will be. And the more intimate our relationship with God, the more our trust and faith in Him will grow.

The people I consider to be people of faith are also people of prayer. They pray as naturally as I drink water when I'm thirsty or sleep when I'm tired. They pray on a regular schedule as well as whenever they have free moments during the day.

To the Thessalonians Paul said, "Pray without ceasing" (1 Thes. 5:17) and to the Ephesians, "With all prayer and petition pray at all times in the Spirit, and with this in view, be on the alert with all perseverance and petition for all the saints" (Eph. 6:18).

Luke commented on Jesus' teaching about prayer, "Now He was telling them a parable to show that at all times they ought to pray and not to lose heart" (Luke 18:1). The Scripture is quite blunt—the person of God is to be a person of prayer.

But how can we pray without ceasing? And what do we pray about? Martin Luther claimed that he spent the first three hours of every day praying. What would we pray about for three hours every day? Wouldn't we run out of things to say?

Have you ever had a reunion with an old friend you haven't seen for some time? A while ago I had lunch with someone I hadn't seen for years. Because we had been good friends and had shared very openly with each other when we worked together, I was sure that we would talk on and on for hours. But in less than one hour, we had about covered everything we wanted to say. We caught up on all the old news, chit-chatted for a while, and then we were done. We ran out of things to say to each other.

On the other hand, my wife and I never run out of things to talk about, even though we see each other every day. There isn't enough time each evening to share everything we've thought about or heard or read or done that day.

Even though much more had transpired in the three years since I had seen my friend than in the eight hours since I last saw my wife, conversation flows much more readily with

Brenda than with my former associate. Why? Because the more time we spend with a person, the more we trust them. The more we trust them, the more we feel free to share everything with them. And as our relationship with a person deepens, we realize that they actually care about anything we say, while acquaintances might not.

In the same way, the more time we spend alone with God, the more we learn to trust Him. The more we grow to trust God, the more free we feel to share everything and anything with Him. The more we pray, the more we have to say to God in our prayers. On the other hand, when God is relegated to the role of an acquaintance who is only consulted on matters of major significance, we will most likely find five minutes more than enough for what we want to say to God.

Make prayer a regular habit. Start by setting aside a daily time when you will spend three minutes just talking to God. After a week of spending three minutes a day praying, begin praying seven minutes a day. At first you might find three minutes to be a long time. Soon, if you're consistent, half an hour won't seem to be nearly enough time. And the more you pray, the stronger your faith in God will become.

Many individuals have shared with me the value of keeping a written record of their specific prayer requests as a means of growing their faith. Our faith grows when we see specific, tangible answers to our specific prayers. Instead of praying, "God, bless my brother," I can pray, "God help my brother to find a job that will make use of his abilities and enable him to be a witness for You." This is a prayer that forces me to stretch my faith. Praying specifically exercises my faith. In the first prayer, I might be able to rationalize anything that happens to my brother as an answer to my request to bless him. But my faith is strengthened far more when I hear that on a specific day my brother began a job that perfectly suits his abilities.

Specific prayer stretches our faith, and specific answers to prayer reinforce our faith. Writing down specific requests and keeping track of the specific answers is an invaluable faith-building tool. Writing our requests forces us to be definite and provides us with a means of verifying that God in His grace has responded to our prayers. Also, by writing our specific requests, we are putting our faith on the line. We are taking a risk, we are stretching ourselves. And faith, like any quality, grows as we stretch it.

Of course, not all prayer is making requests of God, any more than all conversation with my wife is about what happens to me. My wife likes to hear that I love and appreciate her. So does God! Tell God you love Him! Tell Him specifically what you appreciate about Him. Let Him know how wonderful you think He is! We read in Psalm 113:3, "From the rising of the sun to its setting, the name of the Lord is to be praised." Just as the prayer of petition grows our faith, so does the prayer of praise.

Step Three—Corporate Worship

Worshiping God as you pray at home or in your car or at the beach is pleasing to God and valuable for growing your faith. Yet the habit of worshiping God regularly with other believers cannot be neglected without doing significant harm to your faith and the faith of others.

The author of Hebrews challenges us to worship corporately: "And let us consider how to stimulate one another to love and good deeds, not forsaking our own assembling together, as is the habit of some, but encouraging one another" (Heb. 10:24-25). The corporate worship service is a time to praise God, and it is also a time to encourage and motivate each other. As I hear others relate how God has worked in their lives, as I listen to them sing God's praises, as I see them actively commit themselves to God by giving their money, my faith is built up. I am motivated to follow their example and join with them.

A person of faith cannot survive alone. God did not design us to be Lone Rangers. There may be short periods in our lives when we are separated from other believers because of calamity or emergency, but these times are the exception. We Christians need each other, to admonish and challenge (Rom. 15:14), to encourage and comfort, to cry with each other and to share our pain and doubt (1 Thes. 5:11, 14; Rom. 12:10-15). We need others to teach us and to answer our questions (Col. 3:16). Paul explained it this way: "For I want very much to see you, in order to share a spiritual blessing with you to make you strong. What I mean is that both you and I will be helped at the same time, you by my faith and I by yours" (Rom. 1:11-12, GNB).

Faith grows as it is brought into contact with faith. I need your faith to refresh my own when I am dragging spiritually. You need my faith to pick up yours when doubt clouds your skies.

Corporate worship provides us with a regular opportunity to have our faith recharged by the faith of others. It also gives us a chance to hear the Word of God read and explained and applied. It helps us focus on the greatness of God rather than on the difficulty of our problems.

Worshiping with other people is in itself a means of exercising and demonstrating our faith. It is an affirmation that we believe in God and are committed to Him. It is an affirmation of our belief in God's goodness, in the meaningfulness of life, and in the values God has revealed in the Bible. Faith grows when we affirm it, when we renew our commitments, when we ratify our beliefs—particularly when we affirm our faith publicly. There is something about making a commitment in front of other people, whether it involves repeating marriage vows or repeating a statement of faith, that cements our commitment.

These are the basics of growing our faith—studying the Bible, praying, and worshiping corporately. What I've written here is not revolutionary. Yet I know from my own experience that I don't always do what I know I should, and that I need to be reminded over and over again to study God's Word, to pray specifically and consistently, and to worship corporately each week.

I recently heard the story of a man who had just graduated from a prestigious school with an MBA. Being eager to advance in the business world, he went to a high-ranking executive in the company where he had just begun working and asked, "What's your secret? How can I be successful in this business? What's made you so successful?"

The executive paused for a moment, and then revealed his secret of success in one sentence: "I do what you know."

The person who has developed a strong faith does what so many of us know we should do. The secret isn't in knowing we should study the Bible or that we should pray. The secret is in doing what we know we should do.

11 Growing Your Faith—II

Physical exercise has always been an important part of my life, even though I haven't always been as consistent as I would like to be about staying in shape. While I am aware of the benefits of being in condition, I am also quite aware of the effort and pain involved in getting into shape. I know that the price of conditioning is sweat, gasping for air, aching muscles, and exhaustion. The sign that hung in our high school locker room capsulized the unpleasant truth: "No pain, no gain."

Just as getting into physical shape demands discipline and hard work, so does getting our faith into shape. A person doesn't just "happen" to develop a strong faith any more than an athlete "happens" to develop strong muscles, speed, and agility.

Paul challenged Timothy to develop his character: "Train yourself in godliness; for while bodily training is of some value, godliness is of value in every way, as it holds promise for the present life and also for the life to come" (1 Tim. 4:7-8, RSV). To become godly, to develop character, to strengthen our faith, requires training. It involves having a plan and following through on that plan.

So far we have seen that the training program for growing our faith involves three steps—reading and studying the Bible every day; daily, specific prayer; and corporate worship. The following seven steps add muscle to our already strong faith.

Step Four—Study Apologetics

Apologetics is the study of *why* a Christian believes *what* he believes. The word *apologetics* comes from the Greek word *apologia*, meaning "defense." The word is used in 1 Peter 3:15 where we are told, "But sanctify Christ as Lord in your hearts, always being ready to make a defense to every one who asks you to give an account for the hope that is in you." One reason, then, for studying apologetics is because the Bible commands us to always be prepared to give an explanation of our beliefs to those who want to know.

A second reason is that studying apologetics strengthens our faith. The Christian faith is not without reason or against reason. Rather, it is based on reason and on evidence. It is a faith-building experience to discover that there are many good, rational reasons for believing what the Bible teaches.

Here is a sampling of some of the issues in a study of apologetics:

• Does God exist? How do we know? How can we be sure?

• Is the Bible really God's Word? How do we know?

• Did Jesus Christ rise from the dead? Are there any other reasonable explanations for what happened to the body of Jesus?

• Is Jesus Christ God? How do we know?

• Is Jesus Christ the only way to God? What about the other religions—how do we know that they are wrong and Christianity is right?

- Doesn't science contradict the Bible?
- If God is good, how can He allow so much pain and suffering in our world? Why doesn't God put a stop to the suffering of innocent people?
- How can a loving God send people to hell?

For a Christian to ask himself these questions is not sacrilegious. God won't strike us with lightning for searching for the truth. Nor will the foundations of Christianity collapse because someone examines the evidence to find out why Christians believe that Jesus rose from the dead. While there may not be exhaustive answers to every question we can raise, there are reasonable and sufficient answers.

In his book *The Mind Changers*, Em Griffen points out that the best way to prevent a believer from abandoning his faith in God and the Bible is through what he calls "belief inoculation." The analogy is that of giving a person a vaccination. To prevent me from developing smallpox, the doctor scratches a small drop of toxin into my skin. The doctor is actually placing a small dose of the virus itself into my bloodstream so that I will contract a mild case of smallpox, one mild enough so that my body will be strong enough to resist it. In fighting the virus, my body will also develop antibodies that will be available to fight off a stronger attack of smallpox later on. By being exposed to a mild version of the disease, my body has been prepared to defend itself against the real thing. Griffen explains:

> The same is true in the area of beliefs. If we want to help prevent a major shift of attitude away from Christian truth, we need to inoculate a person against falsehood. Pretending it doesn't exist is a mistake. Right now my son believes in the bodily resurrection of Jesus Christ. To him, it's silly to think otherwise. But I need to warn him that many people don't believe in the resurrection, and he should know some of their

arguments. In this way he'll be motivated to ward off their attack, and at the same time he'll have some practice in resisting their persuasion. William McGuire, the founder of inoculation theory, calls this a "vaccine for brainwash" (Tyndale, p. 176).

I have found it best to study apologetics with a small group of committed Christians who are willing to honestly examine the roots of their faith. As we ask questions of each other, we learn how to formulate clearly exactly why we believe what we do. Until we can verbally express something, we probably don't understand it. Studying together forces us to learn to express our beliefs and thus aids us in understanding them better.

A book that has been a valuable resource for me, and which I recommend to groups doing such a study, is *Know Why You Believe* by the late Paul Little. It's straightforward, well-researched, concisely argued, and quite readable. Other resources are more exhaustive, but few are as helpful.

Step Five—Memorize Faith-Inspiring Verses

Faith involves intellect as well as emotions and will. Theologians, philosophers, and psychologists concur on few matters; but one area they do agree on is that the way to change how a person feels and acts is by changing his thinking. Therefore, to strengthen the emotion of faith and to spark faith into action, we must first nourish the mind of faith. One powerful means of feeding the mind of faith is to memorize faith-inspiring verses.

Paul, in writing to the Corinthians, made clear that the battle between faith and unbelief involves our thoughts:

> For though we walk in the flesh, we do not war according to the flesh, for the weapons of our warfare are not of the flesh,

but divinely powerful for the destruction of fortresses. We are destroying speculations and every lofty thing raised up against the knowledge of God, and we are taking every thought captive to the obedience of Christ (2 Cor. 10:3-5).

To the Romans Paul explained precisely how the Christian can be transformed: "And do not be conformed to this world, but be transformed by the renewing of your mind" (Rom. 12:2).

One of the best-selling books of this century is Norman Vincent Peale's *The Power of Positive Thinking.* In it Peale says:

You can think your way to failure and unhappiness, but you can also think your way to success and happiness. The world in which you live is not primarily determined by outward conditions and circumstances but by thoughts that habitually occupy your mind. ... You can make yourself ill with your thoughts and by the same token you can make yourself well by the use of a different and healing type of thought. ... To change your circumstances, first start thinking differently (Prentice-Hall, pp. 169-170).

Dr. David Schwartz affirms Peale's suggestions in *The Magic of Thinking Big:*

When you believe, your mind finds ways to do. When you believe something is possible, your mind goes to work for you to prove why. But when you believe, really believe, something can be done, your mind goes to work for you and helps you to find the ways to do it (Prentice-Hall, p. 72).

Of course, believing something that isn't true is no more helpful than not believing something that is true. Jesus said that the *truth* would set us free. For that reason, it is important to feed our minds the truth about who we are, what we can do, and what is possible through God's power. By memorizing Scripture we nourish our faith with the truth.

By memorizing Scripture we also transform our thinking, and that is the key to transforming our emotions, our actions, and our lives. How we feel is a direct result of what we habitually think about. How we act is a direct result of what we believe. If we tell ourselves over and over again that there is no hope for us, that our lives are a mess, that we're at a dead end, we eventually believe those statements and act on them. But if we persist in telling ourselves that there is always hope, that we are loved by God, and that God can help us begin again, we learn to believe these statements and act on them.

Here are just a few of the verses that would be helpful to memorize:

• "For nothing will be impossible with God" (Luke 1:37).

• "For truly I say to you, if you have faith as a mustard seed, you shall say to this mountain, 'Move from here to there,' and it shall move; and nothing shall be impossible to you" (Matt. 17:20).

• "Be anxious for nothing, but in everything by prayer and supplication with thanksgiving let your requests be made known to God. And the peace of God, which surpasses all comprehension, shall guard your hearts and your minds in Christ Jesus" (Phil. 4:6-7).

• "I can do all things through Him who strengthens me" (Phil. 4:13).

There are many other faith-inspiring verses in the Bible. It is good to say the verses out loud, at least once a day. When we say something aloud we utilize more of our senses and thus reinforce the truth in our minds. Often just saying verses out loud changes how we feel. It's difficult to feel despondent and defeated while you're saying, "I can do all things through Christ who strengthens me!"

To grow your faith, feed your mind daily with faith-inspiring verses. Because those verses contain truth, they have the power to transform your thoughts, your feelings, and your actions. You can develop your own program of Scripture memory, or make use of one of the many good memory programs available at Christian bookstores. Don't wait—get started now! Build your faith by memorizing Scripture!

Step Six—Read Biographies of People of Faith

We are all curious about what other people are really like. That is why *People* magazine and the many tabloids are so popular. They claim to give us the behind-the-scenes stories of celebrities' lives.

Since that curiosity is built in, why not use it to build your faith? Instead of reading about the off-screen exploits of Hollywood's latest stars, go to the library or bookstore for some biographies of great Christians. Read about the martyrs of the early church, about the church fathers who battled heresies, about the leaders of the Reformation who risked their lives to stand up for the truth of Scripture, and about missionaries who have courageously gone to hostile environments to share the Good News.

Read about people of faith and discover what they did to develop their own faith. Learn how they handled their doubts, how they cultivated the strength to persistently trust God even when the mountain came crashing down on them. Read about Augustine, Thomas Aquinas, Martin Luther, John Wesley, D. L. Moody, Adoniram Judson, and others who through their faith made a mark on their world.

Your faith grows as it is exposed to the faith of other believers. To encourage and build up the faith of his readers, the author of Hebrews spent one whole chapter reminding them of the people of faith who had gone before them

(Hebrews 11). Since then, a host of other men and women of faith have walked on this earth. We need to know their stories as well, to expose ourselves to their faith. As we do, our faith will grow.

Step Seven—Nourish Yourself on Positive People and Books

Because our faith is a product of what we feed it, it is important to guard ourselves from influences which are negative. People who are critical, negative, and cynical are not healthy to be around. Just as faith can be contagious, so can negativism and doubt.

Most likely, the people you associate with are a broad mix—some are generally positive, some negative, and some varying according to the weather. You have Christian friends who are people of strong faith, while others give away the weakness of their faith by constantly complaining, criticizing, and generally being grouchy.

Of course, it wouldn't be right to cross off your list everyone who is not positive, hopeful, constructive, optimistic, and full of faith. The Bible commands us to minister to all people, not just those who build us up. We are to be agents of faith and hope to those who are filled with hurt, discouragement, frustration, or bitterness.

At the same time, we must be careful to monitor which direction the influence is flowing. If in your effort to bring sunshine into the life of a negative individual you find yourself consistently influenced by him, most likely you should limit your relationship with that person. He is doing you more harm than you are doing him good.

Make an effort to balance out the amount of time you spend trying to minister to those who are hurting and discouraged by seeking out people who radiate faith. There are some days as a pastor when all I do is try to encourage people who are in some sort of pain. Even though none of them actually intend to sap my energy and hopefulness, a steady diet of hurt and pain can't help but affect my outlook on life. I come away from those days drained and sometimes quite negative.

To protect my reservoir of faith from being depleted, I have learned to take some faith injections regularly by seeking out the company of positive, hopeful, spiritually strong people. I'll call them up on the phone in the middle of the day to hear their cheery voices and to get a dose of optimism. I meet them for breakfast or for lunch to get infected by their energy and enthusiasm. They refresh me, they motivate me, they pick me up. By their faith they wipe the bugs off my windshield and help me to see more clearly the power and grace of God. Their faith is contagious. My faith grows just by being with them.

Make sure you have some people in your life you can depend on to refresh and invigorate you. If you can't think of any, go and find them. They're out there. God has been careful to sprinkle our world with enough Philemons to make sure we have someone to build us up when life tears us down. Ask your pastor to help you find a positive, refreshing person of faith who can infect you with hope. Faith is caught as much as it is learned and developed.

Step Eight—Set Goals

A goal is a statement of faith. It is a statement of how we want things to be at some point in the future. By setting goals for our lives we are viewing ourselves as we *can* be rather than as we are. We are seeing ourselves through the eyes of faith.

We are well aware that significant achievements don't just happen. No one just happens to climb Mt. Everest. No one happens to develop an ability to sing. A happy, harmonious marriage doesn't just happen. We achieve because we set goals, make plans, and take action.

The mountains we face are moved when by faith we visualize those mountains being moved, when by faith we develop a plan to move the mountains, and when by faith we take action.

In their book *Strategy for Living*, Edward Dayton and Ted Engstrom suggest that it is best to set our goals high enough so that we are stretched by them:

> The most effective people are those who set their goals just beyond what they can reasonably expect of themselves. They set moderately difficult but potentially achievable goals. In biology, this is known as the overload principle. In weight lifting, for example, strength cannot be increased by tasks that are performed easily or that cannot be performed without stress to the organism. Strength can be increased by lifting weights that are difficult but realistic enough to stretch the muscles (Regal, p. 44).

To grow our faith, we must stretch it. We can stretch our faith by setting goals that require a bit more of us than we can easily accomplish. To set goals for ourselves—intellectual, physical, educational, financial, spiritual, relational, and vocational goals—is to exercise our faith. To set goals that are just beyond what we think we could reach is to stretch our faith. And that is how faith grows—through exercise and stretching.

Step Nine—Develop an Accountability Group

If you are serious about growing your faith, you need to be in an accountability group. This is a small group of friends who will support you in your effort and who will keep you accountable to your goals.

Training is easier and more productive when it is done with another person. It has always been helpful for me to train for a sport or to study for a class with other people who have the same general goals as I do. To work together toward a goal motivates each person to persevere when the training becomes difficult. It's quite embarrassing to quit when the other three members of the group are still trying. Their persistence challenges me not to give up.

An accountability group also serves as support. The other members of the group help me in dealing with those emotions and events that challenge my faith. When I have doubts, when I am afraid to take a risk, when I'm too tired to go on, they are there to pray with me and to give me courage and hope. When I forget those truths that I believe in, they are there to remind me.

An accountability group functions best when it is small, when it meets weekly, when it provides time to share goals and dreams as well as frustrations, and when the group reads Scripture and prays together. Many people told me in our interviews that praying with other people has a powerful faith-building effect. If you are unable to organize a small group to meet with you, make it a habit to pray with some other person regularly. It will strengthen your faith.

Step Ten—Share Your Faith

Finally, to grow your faith it is imperative to share it. By sharing I mean explaining to others in a caring and persuasive way the truth of the Bible, the good news about Jesus Christ. When you share your faith, you will find that some people will respond positively to your message and commit themselves to Jesus Christ. You will have the thrill of seeing their lives transformed by the power of God.

There have been two points in my life when I had intense doubts about my Christian faith. On both occasions I continued to share my faith even though I wasn't convinced I believed everything I was saying. On both occasions, people accepted Christ as their Lord and experienced dramatic changes in their lives. I couldn't argue with the power of God to change a person, because I had seen it with my own eyes. Each time my faith was significantly restored and I had a growth spurt!

Often though, others will respond to the sharing of our faith with resistance, apathy, or even hostility. Yet those experiences also grow our faith. They make us more resilient, more determined. They challenge us to become more knowledgeable about what we believe so that we can explain the Gospel more clearly and persuasively. They toughen our faith, as heat tempers steel.

Sharing our faith in God with others is risky. But the act of taking a risk is the act which produces growth. Faith that is shared in word and in deed is a faith that grows.

Faith grows as we feed it, nourish it, exercise it, stretch it, share it, and use it. Through our own hard work and willingness to risk, we can take the seed of faith planted in our hearts by God and grow it into a dynamic power capable of effectively healing and transforming our world.

12 Faith Personified

The most effective way for a student to learn a new idea is by example. Math students learn to add and subtract as their teachers demonstrate the process for them on the board. My wife finally succeeded in teaching me to drive a car with a manual transmission by showing me how to do it. If she had simply told me what to do without giving an example, I might still be trying to learn.

Explaining what faith is and how it affects our lives is helpful for us only up to a point. To really understand faith, we need to see it alive in a human body, walking, talking, laughing, and crying. We need to see faith moving the mountain. We need to see it enduring when the mountain refuses to move. We need to see faith refreshing tired, grimy, discouraged people. In order for faith to become more than an idea, it is imperative that we see a living example.

Jesus is that example. He is faith personified. The dictionary defines *personify* as "to typify or embody." To *embody* is "to give bodily form to; to give definite form to." Through the miracle of the Incarnation, God clothed Himself in the human body of Jesus. In so doing, He embodied each of His own moral qualities. Jesus Christ, the God-Man, is the embodiment of love and compassion, righteousness and holiness, and faith.

We have seen that Hebrews 11 is a chapter replete with real-life examples of faith. Hebrews 12 begins by calling our attention to still another example:

> Therefore, since we have so great a cloud of witnesses surrounding us, let us also lay aside every encumbrance, and the sin which so easily entangles us, and let us run with endurance the race that is set before us, fixing our eyes on Jesus, the author and perfecter of faith, who for the joy set before Him endured the cross, despising the shame, and has sat down at the right hand of the throne of God (vv. 1-2).

Jesus is the author and the perfecter of faith. The Greek word *archegos*, translated as "author," is closely related to an Aramaic term for a strong swimmer who was often a member of a crew on an ocean vessel. When a ship was close to land, and the turbulent sea prevented it from getting through the rocks and reefs to shore, this member of the crew would tie a rope around his waist, dive into the sea, and swim to shore. After securing the rope on shore, he would assist the rest of the crew in climbing the rope to safety.

Jesus is the author, the pioneer of faith who went before us to make the path safe. By faith He plunged into the seething sea of sin to secure our deliverance, to set us free from sin's savage power to destroy. As the initiator of faith, Jesus paved the way for us.

Jesus is also the perfecter of faith. The Greek word for "perfecter" is *teleiotos;* it gives the meaning that Jesus has fulfilled or completed faith. He began faith and finished faith. He is both its architect and its constructor. He is the complete embodiment of faith, the one who gives it substance and makes it tangible.

As the embodiment of faith, what was Jesus like? What did He accomplish? What example did He set for us?

Jesus' Faith That Moved Mountains

The Gospel accounts record many of Jesus' miracles. Yet these represent only a sampling of all the wonders Jesus actually performed. In the very last verse of his Gospel, John wrote, "Now, there are many other things that Jesus did. If they were all written down one by one, I suppose that the whole world could not hold the books that would be written" (21:25, GNB).

Just a sampling from Matthew's Gospel yields ample evidence that Jesus had a faith which could move mountains. Within three short years Jesus:
- healed a leper (8:1-4)
- healed the centurion's servant (8:5-13)
- healed Peter's mother-in-law (8:14-15)
- halted an ocean storm (8:23-27)
- healed a demoniac (8:28-34)
- healed a paralytic (9:1-8)
- healed a woman (9:18-22)
- raised a dead child (9:23-26)
- restored sight to the blind (9:27-31)
- healed a man's lame hand (12:9-14)
- healed a blind and dumb man (12:22)
- healed many by the touch of His cloak (14:36)
- fed over 5,000 people with five loaves of bread and two fish (14:13-21)
- walked on water and calmed a stormy sea (14:22-33)

That Jesus was able to move mountains goes without argument. But what most of us wonder is how the miracles that Jesus performed are an *example* to us. After all, an example is something to be imitated. How are we supposed to imitate what Jesus did? Jesus was God, but we are only humans—and that's a big difference!

It is true that Jesus, being both God and man, lived an extraordinary and unique life. Yet the Bible insists that the miracles that Jesus performed were miracles He did as a man, that Jesus did not make use of His power as God to do what He did but rather that He lived as a normal human being, utilizing the power of the Holy Spirit by faith.

Jesus didn't begin His ministry, and never performed a miracle, until He was 30 years old. His public ministry began at His baptism.

> Now it came about when all the people were baptized, that Jesus also was baptized, and while He was praying, heaven was opened, and the Holy Spirit descended upon Him in bodily form like a dove, and a voice came out of heaven, "Thou art My beloved Son, in Thee I am well-pleased." And when He began His ministry, Jesus Himself was about 30 years of age (Luke 3:21-23).

Luke emphasized throughout his Gospel that the source of Jesus' healing power was the Holy Spirit who descended on Jesus at His baptism. According to Luke, the Holy Spirit was the One who led Jesus into the wilderness to fast and to withstand the temptations of Satan (4:1). The Holy Spirit empowered Jesus to teach (4:14-15). The Holy Spirit enabled Jesus to give sight to the blind and to free the oppressed (4:18).

Luke began his account of the healing of the paralytic at Capernaum by saying, "On one of those days, as He was teaching, there were Pharisees and teachers of the law sitting by, who had come from every village of Galilee and

Judea and from Jerusalem; and the power of the Lord was with Him to heal" (5:17, RSV).

In the first few hundred years following the resurrection of Jesus, a constant source of aggravation and opposition for the early Christians was the heresy that Jesus was not God. The Bible makes it plain that Jesus was fully God, that He created the world, that in Him dwelt the full nature of God (Heb. 1:1-4; Col. 1:15-16; 2:9; John 1:1).

Yet it is just as much of a heresy to suggest that Jesus was not fully man, to say that He lived on earth as God and performed His miraculous works only as God. The incarnation of Jesus was not the diminishing of deity but the acquiring of manhood. In Jesus, God became a human being. "Since the children, as He calls them, are people of flesh and blood, Jesus Himself became like them and shared their human nature.... This means that He had to become like His brothers in every way" (Heb. 2:14, 17, GNB).

Jesus was not half God and half man. The Bible insists that Jesus was fully God and fully man. As a human being, He was subject to the same limitations we are. He became tired, thirsty, and hungry. He knew what it felt like to be angry and happy. He was tempted. He worked with His hands.

What does all this have to do with faith? If Jesus lived as a man, He used the same resources that are available to us. "Truly, truly, I say to you, he who believes in Me, the works that I do shall he do also; and greater works than these shall he do; because I go to the Father" (John 14:12).

Luke especially reminded his readers that it was the Holy Spirit who empowered Jesus to preach with eloquence and to heal with proficiency. While you and I are not gifted in the same way as Jesus was, 1 Corinthians 12 affirms that each of us is supernaturally gifted in some way or another to minister to other people's needs. The Spirit that filled, guided, and empowered Jesus of Nazareth is available to do the same for us.

Jesus told His disciples that the reason they failed to heal the epileptic boy was because of the littleness of their faith (Matt. 17:20). By implication, what enabled Jesus to heal the boy was His faith! By faith in the power of the Holy Spirit to operate through Him, Jesus healed the lame and the blind, raised the dead, and walked on the water.

Jesus never used His faith to achieve personal success, to build a reputation, or to accumulate wealth. He used His faith to minister to the needs of others. He didn't use His faith to deliver Himself from the Roman soldiers or to free Himself from the cross. He used His faith and the power of the Spirit to give a mother back her only son, to heal the servant of a compassionate Roman centurion, to restore sight to a blind beggar. Jesus is our example, demonstrating for us how to use the power of the Spirit in faith to compassionately minister to people who hurt.

Jesus' Faith That Didn't Quit

As well as personifying the faith that moves mountains, Jesus also personifies the faith that doesn't quit. Despite the perpetual opposition of the Pharisees and the Sadducees, despite the intense physical pain He suffered, and the persistent antagonism of Satan, Jesus never quit trusting or obeying God the Father. He was faithful to the very end.

Because we believe so strongly that Jesus is God as well as man, it is tempting for us to think that it was easier for Him to resist temptation than it is for us, that the pain Jesus endured wasn't quite as distressing for Him as it would be for us. Yet because Jesus lived on earth as a human being, the temptations He faced were as alluring as those we face. The pain caused by the crown of thorns, and from the nails hammered through the palms of His hands, was as excruciating for Him as it would be for us. And the anxiety and the dread He experienced as He anticipated physical death and separation from His Father—a separation caused by taking our sin upon Himself—was as gnawing and as frightful as anything we have ever experienced.

Matthew's account of Jesus in the Garden of Gethsemane reminds us of the anguish Jesus experienced as He contemplated being crucified for our sins:

> Then Jesus came with them to a place called Gethsemane, and said to His disciples, "Sit here while I go over there and pray." And He took with Him Peter and the two sons of Zebedee, and began to be grieved and distressed. Then He said to them, "My soul is deeply grieved, to the point of death; remain here and keep watch with Me." And He went a little beyond them, and fell on His face and prayed, saying, "My Father, if it is possible, let this cup pass from Me; yet not as I will, but as Thou wilt" (26:36-39).

But Jesus remained faithful. He didn't fold under the pressure of pain. He didn't give in to His fear or His urge to flee. He was faithful even to death.

What can we learn from Jesus' example of faithfulness? First, we are to be faithful to God by our obedience in the face of temptation. Hebrews 4:15 says about Jesus, "For we do not have a high priest who cannot sympathize with our weaknesses, but One who has been tempted in all things as we are, yet without sin." Jesus never gave in to temptation but persisted in living up to God's moral standards. He never gave in to dishonesty, bitterness, gossip, laziness, gluttony, complaining, or selfishness. He remained faithful by persistently obeying God. That is the example we are to follow.

Second, we are to follow Jesus' example in faithfully trusting God in the face of suffering.

For you have been called for this purpose, since Christ also suffered for you, leaving you an example for you to follow in His steps, who committed no sin, nor was any deceit found in His mouth; and while being reviled, He did not revile in return; while suffering, He uttered no threats, but kept entrusting Himself to Him who judges righteously (1 Peter 2:21-23).

Rather than complaining or becoming bitter, lashing out in revenge or berating God, Jesus suffered in silence. He put His trust in God, knowing that one day God would set everything right. Jesus didn't give up, He didn't turn back, He didn't quit. He went right on obeying and trusting God. He went right on ministering to others and letting people know that He cared about them. His resolve to accomplish God's purpose for His life was undeterred.

Jesus is our example. We are called to model His obedience and His willingness to suffer without complaint in order to fulfill God's will.

Jesus' Faith That Refreshed

Jesus is an example to us of the faith that refreshes. By His faith He gave life to people who had walked in death for years. He transformed sinners into men and women filled with hope, with love, and with joy. He gave meaning and purpose to people who drifted aimlessly through life. He resurrected not only the physically dead but also the spiritually dead.

When I ask people what sort of image they have of Jesus' personality, the usual response is that He was serious, somber, intense, and quiet. Perhaps it's only natural for us to perceive Jesus as being quite solemn, since many of the situations He experienced involved serious matters. Healing a lame person was a serious affair. Engaging in debate with cantankerous Pharisees demanded intensity and deep thought. Being tried by Pilate was a dramatic moment.

But that is not the whole picture. The One who came to give us abundant life also knew how to live abundantly. Certainly Jesus had a personality that was attractive and refreshing to others. As the creator of laughter, certainly Jesus knew how to laugh as well as how to make others laugh. Jesus wasn't bland and boring. Rather, He was a person of dynamism, vitality, joy, and enthusiasm.

In fact, the Pharisees criticized Jesus for being too full of life. He enjoyed life so much that they accused Him of being a party person! In reference to their criticism Jesus commented:

> For John the Baptist has come eating no bread and drinking no wine; and you say, "He has a demon!" The Son of man has come eating and drinking; and you say, "Behold, a gluttonous man, and a drunkard, a friend of tax-gatherers and sinners!" (Luke 7:33-34)

It goes without saying that Jesus, who never sinned, was far from a glutton and a drunkard. Yet other passages (see Luke 5:27-34) make it clear that Jesus did go to dinner parties, that He did socialize with people who themselves enjoyed many of the good things of life. In John 2 we read that Jesus turned water into wine at a wedding party. In those times a wedding feast lasted for a week filled with celebrating, eating, laughing, and dancing. And Jesus was right there with the people in the middle of the party.

Jesus knew how to celebrate life! He knew how to enjoy being with people. After all, the reason He came to earth was to initiate relationships with the people He created, to give abundant life to empty souls. Wherever people were—at parties, in the market, in the carpenter shop, at the temple, in the fields—there was Jesus, loving them and sharing the Good News with them. When Jesus told His followers that He had come to give them abundant life, they knew what He meant. They had seen Him live it. They had seen His sparkle, His excitement, His joy, His energy. They had been refreshed by being with Him and they wanted to be just like Him.

How is Jesus an example of the faith that refreshes? He lived life to the brim, loved God, and celebrated His relationships with people. He took every opportunity to explain in terms His hearers could understand that God loved them and was able to heal their hurts and fill their emptiness. He loved people and believed so totally in their value that He was willing to die on the cross for their sins. The people who came into contact with Jesus knew that He believed in them—in their uniqueness, in their worth, and in their potential. He made people feel special. He made them want to be different, to be holy. He made them feel good about themselves. He gave them hope for a better life, for a fresh beginning.

Yet even more than offering life and modeling life, Jesus Christ *is* life. Said Jesus, "I am the way, and the truth, and the life; no one comes to the Father, but through Me" (John 14:6). To be refreshed, to be forgiven, to be given hope and power and energy, take Jesus as Saviour from your sin. Take Jesus as Lord of your life, as Master of your plans and dreams. Let Jesus give you the abundant life He demonstrated and which He offers to all who believe in Him.

13 Five Faces of Faith

Faith cannot exist in a vacuum. It is dependent on the human being for form and function. Faith has being only when it is conceived within an individual. Faith is a word with a face.

In this chapter we will look at five faces of faith. James tells us in his letter that the Word of God is a mirror. Perhaps as you read this chapter and gaze into a portion of God's mirror, you will see a face resembling your own reflected back to you.

Luke's Gospel provides us with a glimpse at a few of the faces of faith. The raising of Jairus' daughter is recorded in Luke 8:40-42, 49-56. The account is briefly interrupted by the narrative of the healing of a woman plagued by a flow of blood for 12 years. As it happened, Jairus' daughter was 12 years old when she became ill.

Let's look at the story as Luke tells it:

And as Jesus returned, the multitude welcomed Him, for they had all been waiting for Him. And behold, there came a man named Jairus, and he was an official of the synagogue; and he fell at Jesus' feet, and began to entreat Him to come to his house; for he had an only daughter, about 12 years old, and she was dying. . . .

While He [Jesus] was still speaking, someone came from the house of the synagogue official, saying, "Your daughter has died; do not trouble the Teacher any more." But when Jesus heard this, He answered him, "Do not be afraid any longer; only believe, and she shall be made well." And when He had come to the house, He did not allow anyone to enter with Him, except Peter, John, and James, and the girl's father and mother. Now they were all weeping and lamenting for her; but He said, "Stop weeping, for she has not died, but is asleep." And they began laughing at Him, knowing she had died. He, however, took her by the hand and called, saying, "Child, arise!" And her spirit returned, and she rose up immediately; and He gave orders for something to be given her to eat. And her parents were amazed; but He instructed them to tell no one what had happened.

The Face of Desperation

The first face of faith we see is that of Jairus. He was a man of great dignity and importance. As a ruler of the synagogue, Jairus was responsible for conducting the synagogue worship service and for selecting those who would lead in prayer, read the Scriptures, and preach. He was likely a man of ample resources and of significant influence in the community.

But Jairus found himself in a situation he never before had faced. His 12-year-old daughter, his *only* daughter was dying, and his wealth, influence, and social standing could do him no good. He had done everything he could to help her. He had taken her to the best doctors and had tried all of the home remedies he knew. He had taken her to the synagogue and prayed to Jehovah for mercy. Nothing had worked.

There didn't seem to be any other possibilities. Jairus was desperate.

There are some people who know well the meaning of desperation. They have tried everything to deal with their problems and their pain, but everything hasn't been enough. On an average day in the United States, 450 people become so desperate that they attempt to commit suicide, and at least 60 of them succeed. Others express their desperation in ways that are less extreme but just as destructive—through alcohol, through psychosis, through anything that offers an escape.

But in Jairus' desperation was born the seed of faith. He had no one else to turn to, and so in the faith of despair he turned to Jesus Christ. He swallowed his pride, threw off his social status, and fell at Jesus' feet to beg Him to save his daughter.

The problem many of us have is that we have never been desperate enough to throw ourselves completely at the feet of Jesus Christ.

As the youngest in a family of three sons, I was often the victim of my brothers' harassment. They particularly took pleasure in pinning me down and tickling me until I thought I was going to explode. Most of the time I was able to slither out of their grasp and escape to safety, but at times I found myself unable to get free. Now the ultimate humiliation, I learned, is not being pinned down and tickled—it is screaming for your mother to help you. A nine-year-old trying to be "macho" just doesn't do that. But when I got desperate enough, when I didn't think I could stand one more tickle, you can bet that I let out my best ear-piercing cry for Mom.

Many of us are hesitant to throw ourselves at the feet of Jesus because it seems to be a sign of weakness. The strong person can do it on his own. He can pull himself up by his own bootstraps. He has his own resources to rely on. The so-called strong person has never had to throw himself at the feet of Jesus because he's never been desperate enough.

But those who consider themselves the strong people are in fact the foolish people. If we are going to get to heaven, we need help getting there. If we're going to be forgiven for our sin, we need some outside assistance. If we're going to live supernaturally, we need help from the supernatural.

To find forgiveness, power, and peace requires that we be desperate enough to throw ourselves in faith at the feet of Jesus and implore Him to help us.

The Face of Factualism

We see a second face of faith in Luke 8:49: "While He was still speaking, someone came from the house of the synagogue official, saying, 'Your daughter has died; do not trouble the Teacher anymore.' "

If there is anyone in this story I can relate to, it's this messenger. I admire him, for I like to think of myself as a factual person. I hope for the best, but I'm willing to accept the cold hard facts of the matter too. But there is a problem with this—the overly realistic person tends to give up too soon. He limits his faith by what he can see with his eyes, can touch and taste and smell and hear. The faith of factualism is a faith calculated solely in terms of human resources.

In 1981, when I was at the Christian Writers Conference at Mt. Hermon, California, I had the opportunity to hear Carolyn Phillips speak. She is the author of *Michelle*, a book about a girl who had to have one of her legs amputated.

The last thing Michelle would have needed after the amputation was to have a factualist sit down and talk with her. He might have said, "Michelle, you have to be factual now. You aren't going to be able to do the things you did before. You won't be able to be active anymore, etc."

Fortunately, Michelle ignored such people and refused to give up. The weekend we were at Mt. Hermon, Michelle was competing in a national ski contest. Not bad for a girl with one leg.

I don't think we need more factualists. There are too many of us already.

The Face of Skepticism

We see a third face of faith in verses 52 and 53: "And all were weeping and bewailing her; but He said, 'Do not weep; for she is not dead but sleeping.' And they laughed at Him, knowing that she was dead" (RSV).

The third face of faith is that of the professional mourner, the professional cynic, the professional doubter. In New Testament times when someone died, professional mourners were hired to weep and cry and mourn for the deceased. Now these professional mourners were laughing out of scorn, ridicule, and cynicism. They had been to funeral after funeral and had seen thousands of dead people. Death was their business. They had seen the girl and they *knew* she was dead! How could this person possibly say that she was only sleeping?

Unfortunately, there are still a few professional mourners in the world today. Oh, they don't get paid for mourning at funerals, at least not in the United States. But they are so used to being negative and cynical and scornful that they've become as skilled as professionals. Show them a new idea and they'll tell you it won't work. If you make a mistake you can be sure they'll be there nipping at your heels, laughing, and telling you, "I told you so." The professional mourner is the person who knows even better than God how things will turn out. If the professional mourner says it can't be done, then it can't be done, and there's no point praying about it or believing any differently.

Do you know why the professional mourner is so negative, so cynical, so convinced that he's always right and that the "impossible" can't be done? Because even when he's wrong, even when the impossible happens, he doesn't see it. Even after Jesus raised this little girl from the dead, the mourners didn't know about it. Jesus told the parents not to tell anyone. Why didn't Jesus want the cynics, the scoffers, to be put in their place? Why didn't He want everyone to know what a fantastic thing He had done? Do you remember what Jesus said in the Sermon on the Mount? He said, "Do not give what is holy to dogs, and do not throw your pearls before swine, lest they trample them under their feet, and turn and tear you to pieces" (Matt. 7:6).

The mourners weren't fit to know about what Jesus had done. They were positive the girl was dead and nothing could change that. They were already convinced that nothing could be done. So let them keep on being cynical and doubting and negative. That's their profession.

I wonder if from time to time some of us don't fall into that trap—we become so cynical and negative that we can't see the great things God is doing. All we see are problems and failures because that's all we're looking for. I wonder sometimes if there haven't been a host of miracles just around the corner from me that I never saw, just because I was sure they wouldn't happen. I can never go back and see what I've missed, but I can make sure that I don't miss any more.

The Face of Jesus
The fourth face of faith belongs to Jesus. When the messenger poured the cold water of factualism over Jairus' desperation, telling him to quit bothering Jesus because time had run out, Jesus was there to intervene. He knew it was still too early to quit! There was still hope! Jesus knew that His Father was able to do more than Jairus could ever imagine.

Jesus didn't just *hope* that everything would turn out for the best—He expected it to. When He heard the realist try to squelch Jairus' faith, He replied confidently, "Do not fear; only believe, and she shall be well" (9:49, RSV).

I must confess to you that I find it very difficult to pray with the kind of faith Jesus demonstrated, with the faith that expects God to answer, completely convinced that God is going to do what I've asked Him to do. I know that God doesn't always do what I ask. But tragically, I tend to conclude that since God doesn't *always* heal, He *never* heals.

Tony Campolo, chairman of the department of sociology at Eastern College, lecturer, and author of *The Success Fantasy* and *The Power Delusion* (Victor), seems to have a theology of healing that is similar to mine. In other words, he believes God *can* heal, but he's not sure just how often God *does* heal in this day and age.

Tony Campolo tells a story about "The Healing of My Theology." He had been speaking at a small midwestern university. After one session a woman walked down the middle aisle carrying a little boy with braces on his legs. When she got to the front of the auditorium, she said that God had revealed to her that Dr. Campolo was going to heal her son. He was flabbergasted, and tried to explain that God gives different gifts to different people, and that he didn't have the gift of healing. But the mother wouldn't leave. She insisted that God had spoken to her, and that was final.

At this point the chaplain took charge. He asked everyone who did not believe that God was going to heal the boy that night to leave. Everyone left except for four Pentecostal students. The four of them, the chaplain, Tony Campolo, and the woman and her son went into the back room. The chaplain anointed the boy with oil, and they began to pray. Dr. Campolo was feeling a bit skeptical and totally out of place. He began a typical ecclesiastical prayer, while the Pentecostals were praying in tongues.

Suddenly, said Dr. Campolo, the room was filled with the Holy Spirit. While he couldn't explain how or why, Dr. Campolo knew that the Spirit was there in power, and suddenly all his doubts about the boy's healing left him. They withdrew their hands from the boy and stepped back to witness his miraculous healing . . . but the boy wasn't healed.

Three years later Dr. Campolo was speaking in St. Louis. After the service the mother of the crippled boy came up to greet him. Hesitantly, he asked how her son was doing. "Why, fine," she replied. "There he is now." Dr. Campolo turned and watched in amazement as her son came running down the aisle to greet him. The mother explained that the morning after they had prayed for her son, the boy's legs began to straighten out, and that within a month he was totally healed. A little boy's deformity was healed and, said Dr. Campolo, a college professor's theology was healed.

The Fifth Face of Faith

What is the fifth face of faith? At the risk of sounding a bit mystical, the fifth face of faith is mine and yours. Faith exists only in human beings. It assumes the face and the personality of the person it resides in. Each of us has a certain kind of faith. Some have a faith born out of desperation. Some have a faith that has yet to grow because they have never been desperate enough. Some have the limited faith of the factualist, while others may have found that their faith has slipped back into the rut of skepticism. And many have a faith that is becoming more and more like the faith personified by Jesus, which moves mountains, never quits, and infects and refreshes tired and discouraged people.

Whatever stage of development your faith might be at today, there is no need to feel guilty or to despair because your faith isn't as strong as you want it to be. If you aren't satisfied with the vitality of your faith, you have cause for celebration! That dissatisfaction will provide you with the motivation you need to grow in your faith.